The Origins of Britain

Britain before the Conquest
An Archaeological History of the British Isles,
c.1500 BC–AD 1066

General Editor: Andrew Wheatcroft

The Origins of Britain

Lloyd and Jennifer Laing

Charles Scribner's Sons

New York

1 3 5 7 9 11 13 15 17 19   I/C   20 18 16 14 12 10 8 6 4 2

Printed in Great Britain
Library of Congress Catalog Number 80–50650
ISBN 0–684–16658–5

Contents

Illustrations

Plates

Maps

Figure

Tables

Acknowledgments

The authors and publishers would like to thank the following institutions and individuals for allowing photographs to be reproduced and for helping in finding suitable photographs: Aerofilms, Plates 5, 48, 52, 53, 61, 99; Brighton Borough Council, Royal Pavilion Art Gallery and Museums, Plates 21, 93; the Trustees of the British Museum, Plates 18, 19, 22, 28, 29, 32, 33, 34, 35, 57, 71, 72, 73, 87, 89, 95, 98, 100, 101, 102, 105, 108; Trustees of the British Museum (Natural History) Plates 6, 8, 13, 14; Dr J. M. Coles, Somerset Levels Project, Plates 36, 37; Dr J. M. Coles, Plate 44; Miss Andrea Crook, Plate 83; Crown Copyright, reproduced by permission of the Scottish Development Department, Plates 43, 59b; Department of the Environment, Crown Copyright: reproduced with permission of the Controller of Her Majesty's Stationery Office, Plates 27, 43, 45, 46, 49, 54, 59, 81, 82, 85, 91; Mr David Longley, Plate 109; National Museum of Antiquities of Scotland, Plates 31, 41, 63, 64, 65, 67, 70, 74, 77, 90, 94, 96, 97, 104, 106, 107; National Museum of Wales, 16 (a) and (b), 17, 62, 75, 110; Professor M. J. O'Kelly, Plates 42, 55, 56; Salisbury and South Wiltshire Museum, Plate 47; Scottish Tourist Board, Plate 79; Dr J. J. Taylor, Plates 68, 69; the Wiltshire Archaeological Society and the Trustees of the British Museum, Plates 86, 92. We would also like to thank Dr J. J. Taylor for allowing material in the collection of the Department of Prehistoric Archaeology, Liverpool University, to be photographed for Plates 23, 30, 88 and 103. The photographs of these and all other unattributed objects, along with plates 1–4 were taken by the Liverpool University Joint Faculty Photographic Service, the objects illustrated being in the possession of the authors.

Our thanks also to Mr Stephen Green for commenting on Chapter 2 and to Mr Hamish Forbes for reading Chapters 3 and 4. Last, we would like to thank Dr J. J. Taylor for reading the manuscript and offering helpful suggestions and criticisms.

Authors' note
The text of this book was completed in the summer of 1978, and, with certain notable exceptions, does not take into consideration anything published subsequently.

The antiquaries – the discovery of Britain before history

The remote past holds an unparalleled fascination. Successive generations of scholars have asked of it questions that were relevant to their own period, and with unfailing benevolence the past has provided suitable answers. These answers have left us with a series of romantic images of the 'ancient Britons' that even the most matter-of-fact scholar will have difficulty in banishing from his mind. In the popular imagination ghostly Roman soldiers and blond Saxons often march in ranks with the 'ancient Britons', for the study of prehistory has had such a chequered development that prehistoric men have become confused not only with each other, but with those from more historic times. It is only within the past few decades that the prehistoric past has begun to take on a more intelligible shape. Within only the last century or so, 'ancient Britons' have been defined from amongst one vast amorphous mass of humanity into those now most famous men of the Stone, Bronze and Iron Ages. It is with the first two of these periods that this book is concerned.

In the light of modern knowledge, it is difficult to believe just how rapidly the sciences (among them the study of prehistory) have developed in the past century and a half. In any modern magazine it is possible to find jokes and cartoons which betray the commonplace knowledge that our early ancestors had no acquaintance with the wheel and used only stone tools. But only 170 years ago few people believed that the first humans in Britain did not know how to work bronze or iron. Science had not been developed, and in this short time-span reports on ancient monuments have progressed from examples such as this:

> and from what remains it appears to have been of a circular form, and to have had a vallum all around it on the high ground, but not on the east side near the water. We picked up a great deal of pottery within the works. (Richard Colt Hoare, describing Durrington Walls henge, 1812)

to tables of data thus:

$$\sqrt{\frac{n_a\,s_a^2\,n_6\,s_6^2}{n_a + n_6 - 2}} \times \sqrt{\frac{1}{n_a} + \frac{1}{n_6}}$$

$$= \sqrt{\frac{(5 \times 1\cdot0816) + (11 \times 0\cdot8836)}{5 + 11 - 2}} \times \sqrt{\frac{1}{5} + \frac{1}{11}} = 0\cdot5607$$

Therefore $t = 2.13/0.5607 = 3.7988$ with 14 degrees of freedom. This is greater than the critical value of t at the 5% level of significance, which is 2.145. Interpolation in the tables of t shows that a difference as great as this or greater could be expected to occur accidentally less than once in 600 times. In this instance therefore, the hypothesis of concentricity must be rejected. (From an appendix to *Durrington Walls* (1971) in which Prof. R. J. C. Atkinson assessed whether mathematics had been used in the laying-out of the site by Neolithic builders.)

Not surprisingly the modern concepts and terminology that attach to British prehistory are confusing to the layman and it is often easier and certainly more romantic to adhere to some of the more picturesque and understandable myths. The difficulties of the study are precisely those which infuse it with a fascination, an aura of the unknown. Where there is no evidence it is easy to let the imagination go riot; where there is little evidence it can be magnified to mean a great deal. What is to stop the most down-to-earth amongst us from musing on the mossy ruins of an ancient burial mound? Certainly not the history books, for prehistoric times have left no written evidence, few illustrations and a pathetically limited variety of objects or sites. Even the reports of the most advanced analysis can often leave the lay reader none the wiser, for pages of computer data or stat-istics still require some sort of intelligible interpretation and do not 'speak for themselves'.

Yet despite the unavailability of the evidence, it was in the prehistoric past that some of the most revolutionary discoveries and inventions were made. Until the period covered after page 141 of this book for instance, no one in Britain possessed a wheel to help them to haul home deer carcasses or erect monuments. Until nearly the end of the period covered by this volume no one had mounted a horse with any provable degree of success. People hunted fleet wild animals and actually exterminated bison *on foot*. The first people to live in Britain, literally the first ancient Britons, far from wearing woad and brandishing swords, not only were unable to work metal but did not know that if you plant a seed in warm sunny soil and water it, you will end up with a handy source of a meal. Nor had they hit on the simple idea of chasing a collection of animals into an enclosure so they would be on the spot, ready for slaughter if the fish burnt or the meat was 'off'. It took over 3 million years from the time that men first stood upright until they realized that it was more efficient to have meat and cereal on the doorstep instead of having to run miles for a meal.

Much can be discovered from the archaeological evidence. We can describe in accurate detail the sort of weather prehistoric man had to contend with, or the kind of food he enjoyed. We know an appreciable amount about his physical life – his houses, tombs, temples and villages. But of the everyday lives and loves of the ancients we can determine relatively little. By the time, for instance, that young men were shunning hunting as a lifetime occupation and were taking to farming, people in Britain had developed the custom of building tombs for their dead. To judge from the flimsy evidence that remains, they had also worked out lores and rituals connected with burial. But we can do no more than the first antiquaries and make informed guesses as to what these may have been. How did charred bones and broken pottery arrive in the long dank passages of chambered tombs? Was there chanting and dancing, orgiastic ritual and day-long feasting which resulted in these remains? Or did the mourners merely take the opportunity of disposing of their household rubbish with the dead person?

In recent years the British prehistoric past has fallen into perspective, though the legacy of the first antiquaries as well as the sophistication of modern techniques of data recovery has left the learned literature a jungle of jargon and disconnected facts. Yet the countryside is littered with monuments and reminders of the first ancient Britons. The soil in certain areas is sprinkled with their tools and implements. Particularly in the more remote areas where modern development has not destroyed them, barrows, standing stones, tombs and circles shadow the evening grass as they have done for millennia. Under fields and woods lie the remains of settlements where people sewed leather, scraped hides, scratched pictures on bones and gutted fish. The air around the great monuments positively reverberates with the cries of antiquaries, scholars, cranks, teachers, scientists and romantics. Thus the picture we have of the past often tends to become a bizarre mixture of scientific fact and artistic interpretation. The prehistoric past reveals archaeology at its most characteristic.

The growth of knowledge about the prehistoric past

There is no real evidence to show that ancient man was himself interested in his remote ancestors, nor indeed that he had any concept of the antiquity of his species. 'Antiquities' have been discovered on archaeological sites, but they may have been collected either as curiosities or because there was an immediate use for them. A Palaeolithic tool, for instance, was unearthed at the much later site at Thatcham, Berkshire, and had certainly been at least remarked on by the Mesolithic inhabitants there. Mesolithic tools were used during the Dark Ages on a number of settlements. The presence of very old objects on less ancient sites can be explained in numerous ways that do not include an avid interest in history on the part of the ancient finders.

Discoveries of prehistoric antiquities have barely been mentioned in literature – if any explanation were forwarded, it was likely to involve something of a miraculous nature. Thus did the thirteenth-century monk Ralph of Coggeshall ascribe mammoth bones to a dead giant. It was not until the Renaissance that the prehistoric past began to excite curiosity; and the past was full of uncertainties, inaccuracies and dark holes. In Britain this thirst for knowledge did not become widespread until Tudor times. History books explained the coming of the Romans to the Elizabethans and gave them the outline of subsequent events, but the past before 55 BC was shrouded in mystery. It is not without some justification that the modern phrase 'it is positively prehistoric' as used in popular parlance has become infused with even greater connotations of squalor, primitiveness and unknown hardships than its sister phrase 'out of the Dark Ages'.

The ninth-century monk Nennius had confused history for the Tudors by stating that Brutus, grandson of Aeneas (of Roman legendary fame), had settled in Britain in the 'third age of the world'. In the twelfth century Geoffrey of Monmouth engagingly defined the landing-place of this migrant from myth as Totnes. If this classically based story did not appeal, Elizabethans could adhere to the belief that the British derived from the Biblical sons of Japhet, or the Ten Lost Tribes of Israel.

An enterprising Elizabethan headmaster, John Twyne, is responsible for introducing to British history some of the most famous early visitors – the Phoenicians. Twyne was the first to suggest that these traders came to Cornwall seeking tin (a myth which is still surprisingly widely believed despite the absence of any evidence). To support his theory he ingeniously suggested that the Welsh word *caer* (which in fact means a fort and is derived from the Latin *castrum*) was of Phoenician derivation, and that the Welsh women owed their unusual costume to the influence of these traders (it is now thought that the costume is based on English medieval court dress).

A more scholarly-based beginning was made when a certain William Leland was commissioned by Henry VIII to 'peruse and diligently to serche al the libraries of monasteries and colleges of this yowre noble reaulme' for information on British antiquity. He travelled around the country and from time to time described the visible monuments – Hadrian's Wall, Offa's Dyke and the Devil's Arrows, for example. But there was no means at this time of proving the age of the structures. Leland died insane with his book unpublished, but not forgotten, for it proved a basis on which William Camden, probably the greatest of all the early antiquaries, could build.

The son of a painter, William Camden was born in 1551. He attended St Paul's School and Oxford University but was forced to leave the latter without a degree in 1571 after becoming involved in a religious dispute. It is an interesting observation on his character that the university later failed to persuade him to accept an MA degree, on the grounds that he had 'established his reputation upon a better bottom'.

For three years after 1571 Camden travelled around Britain making notes on antiquities. He was sponsored by the famous Elizabethan poet Sir Philip Sidney and two scholars, Gabriel and Godfrey Goodman. At the end of the period he was found a post as second master in Westminster School. There he stayed for the next twenty-three years, though teaching boys was not entirely to his taste – 'the bent of his own genius was always pulling him out, to stately Camps and ruinous Castles, those venerable Monuments of our Forefathers'.

By 1577 his knowledge of British antiquities was famous. In that year the geographer and map-maker Abraham Ortelius came to England and discussed the country's topography with him. He persuaded Camden to set his learning down in book form. Camden's *Britannia* was thus conceived – a work that influenced thought on British antiquity for the next 250 years, and which was frequently reprinted in enlarged editions for generation after generation of scholars. The first edition appeared in Latin in 1586, the fruit of nine years' labour. It was conceived as an account of Roman Britain, but aspects of the prehistoric past inevitably crept in. A fine engraving of Stonehenge, for instance, appeared in the edition of 1600, in which it was described as '*insana substructio*' (a 'mad construction') and in which Camden brought up the now inevitable question of how the monument was built.

The difficulties under which antiquarians were working are illustrated by Camden's suggestion that the stones of the circle were 'artificially . . . made of fine sand cemented together by a glewy sort of matter'. The difference between man-made and natural materials had not yet been determined.

1 William Camden (1551–1623), as he appears on the frontispiece to the 1695 (Gibson's) edition of the *Britannia*. Camden was one of the pioneers of archaeology in Elizabethan England, and his *Britannia* enjoyed wide popularity to the end of the eighteenth century

Studies of prehistoric man at this time were indistinguishable from those of natural phenomena. Consider the resoundingly meaningless pronouncement of Camden's near-contemporary Tollius, who decided that some tools were clearly 'generated in the sky by a fulgurous exhalation conglobed in a cloud of circomposed humour'. Sir William Dugdale came nearer the truth when he asserted that flint implements were 'weapons used by the Britons before the art of making armour of brass or iron was known'. But there was no means of deciding at this period whether Dugdale was correct, or whether it was better to believe the rival opinion that flint implements were thunderbolts made by the little people to throw at cattle.

2   This picture of Stonehenge by Kip adorned the 1695 edition of Camden's *Britannia*, and has all the ingredients of a Dutch landscape. Notice the skulls and bones being unearthed in the bottom left, and the crossed bones and hourglass in the bottom centre, a cautionary reminder of the transience of human existence. This is typical of the best of seventeenth-century antiquarian illustration

The seventeenth century

Some notable advances were made in the careful recording of field monuments during this century. Among the leading figures was John Aubrey (1626–97). He is best known for his *Brief Lives*, which were not published until 1898, though extracts had appeared in print before. They are gossiping accounts of his contemporaries which were successfully adapted for the London stage a few years ago. However, his claim to archaeological fame rests in his more staid *Monumenta Britannica* (unpublished until 1978 and then only in a limited fascimile edition). Aubrey studied Stonehenge and Avebury carefully and came to the measured but uninformative conclusion that both were the work of the 'ancient Britons'.

A younger contemporary of Aubrey was Edward Lhwyd (1660–1708), keeper of the recently founded Ashmolean Museum in Oxford. He travelled extensively and for Edmund Gibson's 1695 edition of Camden's *Britannia* he contributed useful notes on Wales, including the first accounts of the early Christian memorial stones. In Ireland Lhwyd visited the Neolithic chambered tomb of Newgrange and here learned that a coin of the fourth-century Roman emperor Valentinian had been found near the top of the mound. From this he rightly deduced that the mound was built in a period before the Romans, and was therefore the burial place of the 'ancient Irish'.

Neither Aubrey nor Lhwyd, however, was able to define the terms 'ancient Britons' or 'ancient Irish'.

Accurate studies were not aided by an ingenious calculation by James Ussher, Archbishop of Armagh, which had a long-term effect on the view people had of the past. At this point in time the Bible was regarded as incontrovertible fact. The Good Book was particularly clear on the events of the Creation – God created the earth and all on it in six days. Man was conjured up on the sixth day. To set the Creation into some sort of chronological perspective, Ussher endeavoured to assign a date to it. From the records in the Bible that Adam lived to be 930 and that seven generations later Methuselah died at the ripe old age of 969, with his grandson Noah passing on at a youthful 950, the archbishop calculated the year of the Creation. The magical date was 4004 BC. A successor of his, Dr John Lightfoot, narrowed the time down to 9 a.m. on 23 October for the Creation of Adam. Such a precise calculation could hardly be argued with and was accepted without question (it can still be seen printed in the margins of some modern Bibles).

Around 4000 years then, separated Adam from Julius Caesar and the Roman period in Britain. It was ample time in which to fit a procession of Druids, Phoenicians, the Lost Tribes of Israel, the Greeks, and the Trojans. Unfortunately the influence of the calculations held back studies since even in the face of hard proof that man had walked the earth many years before 4004 BC, scholars were unwilling to admit the possibility.

It was inevitable that amongst the wild surmises some would reach nearer the truth, but no one noticed that the right path to follow existed and the possible lines of enquiry were ignored. One such pointer was the finding at the end of the seventeenth century of a flint axe which was associated with elephant bones, at Gray's Inn Lane in London. The finder was an apothecary and antique dealer called Conyers. Conyers suggested that it had been made at a time when Britons did not have any knowledge of metal, but such an idea seemed preposterous. The find was dismissed as the remains of an elephant brought over by Roman emperor Claudius, and the weapon of an ancient Briton of the time.

The eighteenth century

This period began in a flourish of archaeological studies with the career of William Stukeley, but went out with a mist of dilettante musings on the romance of ancient ruins and grinning skulls.

3 A portrait of William Stukeley (1687–1765), adorning a classical column base on the frontispiece to his charming *Itinerarium Curiosum* (1776). Note the Roman coins in the foreground. Stukeley was one of the best but most eccentric of the eighteenth-century English antiquaries. He invented the period's obsession with druids

9

Stukeley epitomizes the best and worse of his century's craze for antiquarianism. He was at once one of the most astute observers and interpreters of the field monuments of the English countryside, and an obtuse romantic, his head filled with some of the most absurd fantasies of the age. Stukeley's particular fancy was for druids – a preoccupation that was so marked amongst some of his contemporaries that it has aptly been named 'druidomania'. He was born in 1687 and was educated at Cambridge where he read medicine. Early on he met Isaac Newton, and read the manuscript of Aubrey's *Monumenta Britannica* which inspired him with an enthusiasm for antiquities. Between 1719 and 1725 he surveyed Stonehenge and Avebury and travelled Britain from Dorset to Hadrian's Wall. His first book, illustrated with his own drawings, was the delightful *Itinerarium Curiosum*, first published in 1724. This mixes archaeological observations with personal anecdote.

Stukeley made three valuable contributions to the study of archaeological remains which seem in retrospect to be remarkably obvious. He was the first to point out that field monuments could belong to a period of time long before the coming of the Romans, that there may have been prehistoric invasions of Britain from the Continent, and that it was more profitable to study groups of monuments than to observe them individually.

In 1729 Stukeley abandoned medicine and, somewhat surprisingly considering his interest in the pagan druids, entered the Church. Before this step he had been toying with the idea that druids built Stonehenge, but once he had taken Holy Orders the ancient priestly caste took on a new reality for him – everything started and ended with the druids. His ideas about them became confused with his religious views in the most extraordinary manner. To him the druids were 'of Abraham's religion entirely' and their faith was so akin to that of Christianity that 'it differed only in this: they believed in a Messiah who was to come into this world, as we believe in him that has come'. He did however admit that 'we cannot say that Jehovah appeared personally to them'. He took to writing what he called 'Vegetable Sermons' which were designed to show the wonderful works of God as illustrated by vegetables. Druids also crept into the homilies. This was in the 1760s when Stukeley's *Stonehenge* (1740) and *Abury* (1743) had already appeared as the first parts of a dauntingly entitled work he had planned – *Patriarchal Christianity, or a Chronological History of the Origin and Progress of True Religion, and of Idolatry*. From this time on Stonehenge and the druids were inseparable in the minds of the general public, and have remained so to the present day. For the rest of the century, antiquarian thought was carried aloft on a wave of soft primitivism and romanticism that lapped against the walls of Gothick ruins, well typified by Stukeley's off-duty moments.

In 1754, for example, Stukeley visited the Princess Dowager in Kent House where they discussed a late Bronze Age hoard of tools which were (of course) pronounced druidical. Stukeley picked up an oak branch in the garden which he felt was symbolic of the occasion, since this tree was supposedly sacred to the druids. While passing the house of a friend, a Mrs Pierson, he decided to send a servant in with an oak bough – 'a present from the royal Archdruidess to her sister Druidess'. Later that night he dined with 'My Lord Archdruid Bathhurst'. When Stukeley came to the scholarly task of classifying barrows he refered to them as 'Kings' barrows', 'archdruid's barrows' and 'priestesses' barrows', while what are now known to be Bronze Age axes were to him, more picturesquely, the hooks used by druids to pull down mistletoe from sacred groves.

Yet hidden in many such fantasies and obscurities were the seeds of the discipline that became the eminently re-spectable and prosaic study of modern prehistory. Had it not been for men like Stukeley and Camden interest in the past might not have been kindled. With every wrong answer they found, questions were asked that eventually led to the correct solutions.

Stukeley made a further positive contribution to the study of the past by his excavations. Until this time, few people had dug holes in the ground for antiquarian reasons, though some burial mounds had been pillaged for possible loot. Stukeley excavated one of the barrows near Stonehenge and made the famous observation that it contained 'bits of red and blue marble chippings of the stones of the temple'. By such an unscientific and simple statement he proved that his barrow was built at the time of the erection of the so-called 'bluestones' of the monument. It was a revolutionary con-clusion for the time, and shines like a fog lamp in the mists of dilettantism.

Barrow digging became a popular sport by the later eight-eenth century, though many mounds belonged not to pre-history but to the Saxon or Roman periods. James Douglas was one of the first to draw ground plans of the barrows he dug up; he published them in his *Nenia Britannica*. He, like Stukeley, was a man of his age. He too went into the Church, seeing this as an ideal occupation for one of anti-

11

quarian tastes. He was obviously not a cleric to be trifled with – he records that he was once hurried from a meal by three Irish soldiers who reported that they had found the bones of a giant. On finding that the skeleton was of normal size the reverend gentleman relates:

> I seized a thigh-bone from the grave, and after having made one fellow stand erect to measure it by his own, I belaboured the fellows with it for their natural promptness to magnify these casual discoveries into the marvellous. It cured my spleen and I returned in better humour, though somewhat disappointed, to my friends.

If such behaviour towards both the diggers and finds were common, it is not surprising that to many seventeenth- and eighteenth-century minds the antiquarian was an object of fun. In *Microcosmographie or a Piece of the World Discovered in Essays and Characters*, published in 1628, John Earle gives this caricature of an antiquarian which, it is to be feared, might well be recognized today.

> He is one that hath that unnatural disease to be enamoured of old age and wrinkles, and loves all things . . . the better for being mouldy and worm-eaten. . . . A great admirer he is of the rust of old monuments, and reads only those characters where time hath eaten the letters. He will go you forty miles to see a saint's well or a ruined abbey; and there be but a cross or a stone foot-stool in the way, he'll be considering it so long, till he forgets his journey. . . . He never looks upon himself till he is grey-haired, and then he is pleased with his own antiquity.

There are echoes here of the opinion of the wife of a modern archaeologist who pointed out that the older an archaeologist's spouse grows the more interested in her he is likely to become.

A popular joke with eighteenth- and nineteenth-century novelists was the antiquary who mistook something modern for a genuine antiquity. Mistakes were pounced on with as much glee as those of a modern music or wine buff. Sir Walter Scott made Jonathan Oldbuck, the hero of *The Antiquary* (1816), discourse at length upon a supposed Roman fort only to be told by a beggar that he remembers the 'praetorium' being built.

The nineteenth century
During this century the study of prehistory took shape, due to discoveries in several fields of knowledge. However, there were also set-backs. For instance, the period 1840–70 was the golden age of barrow looting. Local societies arranged 'excavations' for the Sunday afternoon enjoyment

of their members who frequently included ladies. Indeed, archaeological studies have always offered equal opportunities to those females who have the stamina to compete. In 1870 J. H. Parker informed the Oxford Architectural and Historical Society that 'to find out whether a young lady knows anything of Archaeology or not, is a test whether she has been highly educated or not. The daughters of our higher nobility . . . are almost always well acquainted with Archaeology. Some of my favourite pupils have been young ladies of this class, our future Duchesses or Countesses.'

However, barrow digging could be as tedious for the diggers as reading most of the accounts of it can be for the modern scholar. Thomas Wright records an unrewarding afternoon in 1854 in which, after procuring a plentiful supply of provisions for picnicking, 'we all felt somewhat of a disappointment as our men laboured hour after hour, and no sepulchral chamber presented itself, and not even a burial-urn could be found to reward our patience'. But all enjoyment was not lost on this occasion, as they contrived to pass the time between eating and digging 'in games of various descriptions – not exactly such as those with which the builders of the mound celebrated when they laid the deceased on his funeral pile – and in other amusements'.

Alas for these particular diggers, however, the barrow caved in on them (as any modern excavator might have predicted with all the activity near the edge of the trench) and one of the workmen was nearly killed, no doubt bringing at least some dramatic relief to the afternoon's proceedings and saving an otherwise tedious day from total waste.

From the preceding paragraphs it will not surprise the modern reader to discover that the beginnings of modern archaeological studies in the nineteenth century possibly owed more to the concurrent development of science than to the work of antiquaries. When the century opened the studies were still dilettantism but by its close prehistoric archaeology was a subject in its own right – its framework was understood and excavation techniques had advanced well beyond leisure-time hackings. The key to understanding the past was found not in the musings of the 'druidomaniacs' but in scientific studies.

One of the chief problems still remained – how to explain the presence of fossils of both extant and extinct animals in rocks. In a work entitled *Natural Theology* published in 1802, William Paley reiterated Archbishop Ussher's theory and summed up the past by saying that the world had been created 6,000 years before by God the arch-watch-maker.

He asserted that the story of Genesis and the Flood were historical facts.

Despite the general acceptance, even at this late date, of Ussher's dates, some scholars were having doubts. Only two years before the publication of *Natural Theology* John Frere had sent a letter to the Society of Antiquaries concerning some flint implements found at Diss in Norfolk. He observed that

> They are, I think, evidently weapons of war, fabricated and used by a people who had not the use of metals . . . the situation in which these weapons were found may tempt us to refer them to a very remote period indeed, even beyond that of the present world.

The tools which Frere had found were lower Palaeolithic hand-axes of the type known as Acheulian and they had turned up in undisturbed gravel associated with the bones of extinct animals.

So far as most opinion was concerned, this and other discoveries of stone tools associated with the bones of extinct animals must have been the result of chance – it was just not possible that they could be contemporary. The answer to the problems was the Diluvial Theory – these were the remains of animals drowned in Noah's Flood. There were flaws in the argument – for example different rocks contained different fossils and the older or lower the rocks, the more primitive the fossils were seen to be. Yet some were of creatures still in existence – how could this be if they were swept away in the Flood?

Cuvier solved this with the Catastrophe Theory which stated that there were many natural catastrophes of which Noah's Flood was but one. In each disaster all living things were destroyed and God replaced them with better creatures. This still did not explain why some fossils were of extant creatures, but most people were willing to turn a blind eye in the interests of theological orthodoxy.

It is not surprising that Cuvier was acquainted with the English Dean Buckland. They had in common their personal eccentricities as well as an avid interest in fossils. The story is told how Cuvier awoke one night to see the Devil standing by his bedside (in fact one of his students dressed up). 'Wake up thou man of catastrophes. I am the Devil. I have come to devour you,' announced the visitor. 'I doubt if you can,' replied Cuvier. 'You have horns and hoofs. You only eat plants.'

Buckland's knowledge of natural phenomena was extraordinary too. He is recorded as becoming lost at night when travelling from Oxford to London. Stooping down he picked up a handful of soil, sniffed it and pronounced 'Uxbridge'. He was right. His dinner parties were notorious for the bizarre dishes he served – pickled horse's tongue, grilled alligator and panther chops. Ruskin once escaped from a breakfast of mice on toast though he had enjoyed his evening meal which had been guarded from flies by two Carolina lizards. But as a geologist Buckland was less eccentric. He demonstrated the existence of an Ice Age in Britain, for instance, introduced guano as fertilizer, and became involved in the investigations into early cave deposits and thus in the antiquity of man. At Kirkdale Cave in Yorkshire he found the remains of hyenas, reindeer, tigers, elephants, rhinos and cave bears. He argued that this was evidence for the prevalence of Arctic conditions in Britain (the Ice Age). He carried out an excavation in the Goat's Hole Cave at Paviland on the Gower Coast of Glamorgan. The remains of a young man (he thought it was a female and called it the Red Lady of Paviland as the body had been smeared with ochre) were associated with what we now know to be upper Palaeolithic implements and similar animal bones to those in the Kirkdale Cave. However, Buckland was near to a breakthrough in knowledge but unfortunately refused to believe that Man could be as old as the geological context of the bones and so dismissed the Red Lady as Romano-British.

The breakthrough came in 1859. In 1838 a customs official called Jacques Boucher de Crèvecouer de Perthes had displayed some flint tools that he had collected in the Somme gravels at Abbeville and which he called *haches diluviennes* – 'axes of the Flood'. By 1847 he was convinced that the association between axes and bones of extinct animals was not fortuitous. He considered them to be contemporary, and he published his conclusions in the first part of a three-volume work, *Antiquités celtiques et antédiluviennes*, for his axes seemed to him clearly older than the Flood. Boucher de Perthes managed to persuade learned opinion in France, and soon his findings were reported in England. Two eminent scholars, John Prestwich and John Evans, went to Abbeville to see de Perthes and the scene of his discoveries. After weighing up the evidence they were convinced he was right.

John Evans dominates British prehistory in the mid-nineteenth century. He had married into the John Dickinson paper manufacturing firm and was a successful business-man. His leisure was devoted to the study of antiquities and to the formation of an outstanding collection of prehistoric tools and coins. In many respects he was a pioneer – he was the first to realize the importance of coin hoards both for the numismatist and archaeologist, and was the first to study distributions and to make a proper assessment of the coins of the Iron Age Celts in Britain. His *Ancient Bronze Implements of the British Isles* is still a classic. He had, too, a distinguished son, Sir Arthur Evans, the discoverer of the Minoan civilization of Crete.

Sir John was quick to appreciate the implications for British archaeology of Boucher de Perthes's discoveries. Even as axes were being unearthed at Abbeville, an enthusiastic headmaster William Pengelly had been excavating in Kent's Cavern, Torquay, and in the nearby Windmill Hill Cave at Brixham. In the latter cave he found incontrovertible evidence in support of Boucher de Perthes's theories – flint implements were discovered with the bones of extinct animals *under* a layer of stalagmite from three to eight inches thick. Lying within and on top of the layer of stalagmite itself were the bones of hyena, lion, bear, mammoth, rhinoceros and reindeer. Evans told the Society of Antiquaries on 2 June 1859 that it had apparently been established beyond any doubt that Man peopled Britain in a period of antiquity 'remote beyond any of which we have hitherto found traces'.

Charles Lyell, whose *Principles of Geology* (1830–3) had pioneered the acceptance of the great antiquity of the earth, endorsed Evans's pronouncement. The great antiquity of Man was established – but how ancient might Man be? This question was asked and is still being posed. Further evidence was not slow in coming forward, however, though not in Britain.

In 1859 nearly all the clues to the antiquity of man took the form of flint implements; no really early human fossil had come to light. Two years before, however, one important and now famous hominid fossil had been unearthed at Neanderthal in Prussia – the skull cap and the long bones of what the discoverer regarded as 'the most ancient memorial of the early inhabitants of Europe'. Most people disagreed, however, regarding Neanderthal man as a pathological idiot of no great age. Professor Mayer of Bonn suggested ingeniously that the remains were of a Mongolian Cossack on his way through Prussia in 1814 in pursuit of Napoleon's army. This supposed unfortunate had taken shelter in the cave in which he was found, in order to rest as a result of the pain he was suffering from advanced rickets. The agony had caused the pronounced ridge furrows apparent on the brow ridges of the bones. An earlier discovery of Neanderthal remains at Gibraltar had gone virtually unnoticed.

But within a couple of years of the general acceptance of Man's antiquity the situation had changed. In 1868 some workmen cutting a railway line through the cliffs of Les Eyzies in south-western France came upon a rock shelter at Cro-Magnon which contained the remains of five humans. The discovery gave its name to Cro-Magnon Man, who differed little from his modern descendants. The find showed that by the last Ice Age *Homo sapiens* ruled the earth and that his ancestors had to be sought in a more remote period still. Within a few decades the entire frame of reference in which the past was viewed had become obsolete.

'The Origin of Species'

The year 1859 was of immense importance for the study of ancient man, not only for the address given by Evans to the Society of Antiquaries, but because in this year one of the most celebrated scientific tomes of all time, Charles Darwin's *The Origin of Species*, was published. This book was not specifically concerned with human origins, for not until 1871 did Darwin feel confident enough to suggest that man was descended from ape stock.

Darwin, the son of a doctor, was born in 1809 in Shrewsbury in the Welsh Marches. He began his academic career by studying medicine at Edinburgh University, but found it uncongenial – he preferred 'idle sports' such as shooting and dabbling in natural history. He then went to study divinity at Cambridge but still failed to make much academic headway. Here, however, he met Professor J. S. Henslow, the botanist, who found him a job as naturalist on HMS *Beagle*, which was bound for a five-year voyage round the world. Darwin was ill-equipped for his task, having no scientific training, but was little daunted. On 27 December 1831 he set out, and began making the notes which were to crystallize into his epoch-making theory. Beset with sea-sickness and other illnesses, Darwin collected, observed and pondered. In the Galapagos islands, several hundred miles west of Ecuador, he noticed that not only did each island appear to have its own type of finch, but that different types of the bird were to be found in different environments on the same island. All, however, were clearly of the same stock. Darwin's ideas on natural selection took shape, but he was not to give them voice for some time.

On his return to England he began to make notes for a lengthy work to be entitled *Transmutation of the Species*. He could see that species of animals changed – but why? He suspected natural selection to be the answer. On 3 October 1838 the key came to him while reading Malthus's theories about population. Malthus had propounded the idea of 'Nature's Feast' – that Nature restricts population by letting some starve, otherwise the population would increase in geometric progression. Darwin concluded that changes that were favourable to the survival of a creature would allow it to flourish, while those with less favourable mutations would die out. He wrote a summary of his conclusions, then turned his attention to the study of barnacles.

Encouraged by his friends, in 1856 he began a huge work on natural selection. In 1858 he heard that Alfred Russel Wallace, the explorer and naturalist, had also been reading Malthus and had his mind on the same idea of natural selection. It forced Darwin's hand. Together Wallace and Darwin communicated their theory to the Linnaean Society. It went almost unnoticed. Darwin was now obliged to cut short his prolonged research and publish his results, which he did in 502 pages. The first printing (1,250 copies) sold out on the first day.

Despite his careful avoidance of a discussion of the descent of Man, his ideas provoked a storm. Darwin went into retreat following the publication of his book, and it was left to the naturalist T. H. Huxley to fight for Darwin's case. He came into conflict with the establishment, personified by Bishop Samuel Wilberforce, at a meeting of the British Association for the Advancement of Science at Oxford in 1860. Wilberforce, a distinguished speaker, carefully demolished Darwin's theory. Then he said to Huxley, 'And you sir, are you related to the ape on your grandfather's or grandmother's side?'

'The Lord hath delivered him into mine hands,' murmured Huxley. After presenting the counter-argument to Wilberforce's he concluded, 'A man has no reason to be ashamed of having an ape for a grandfather or a grandmother. If I had the choice of an ancestor, whether it should be an ape, or one who having scholastic education should use his logic to mislead an untutored public, and should treat not with argument but with ridicule the facts and reasoning adduced in support of a grave and serious philosophical question, I would not hesitate for a moment to prefer the ape.'

Darwin's theory had won that round, though there were other battles to be fought before it finally gained universal acceptance. However, it opened the door through which archaeological and especially prehistoric facts could flood. By the late nineteenth century the idea that man evolved over an unspecified but immense length of time, rather than since 4004 BC, was accepted.

The Three Age system

The facts would have been totally unsorted and jumbled, however, had it not been for the efforts of a young man called Christian Thomsen, the first curator of the National Danish Museum. In 1816, faced with the task of arranging the galleries into some semblance of order, he had noticed that on some sites only stone tools were found, while on others there were bronze and stone but none of iron. He reasoned that where metal was lacking it was because people did not know how to use it. Thence it was a short step towards arguing that since bronze is easier to work than iron the use of the materials must have occurred in the order Stone, Bronze and Iron. The Three Age system of partitioning the past had been invented. The museum guide-book became the medium for explaining the concept, which rapidly caught on. The idea was translated into English in 1848 and by the middle of the century antiquaries everywhere were familiar with the terms Stone Age, Bronze Age and Iron Age. The model was technological – it applied simply to the material used for edge tools – and not until the twentieth century was it refined and given wider economic undertones.

Meanwhile, two new terms were coined to divide the Stone Age. Sir John Lubbock (Lord Avebury) first used the term Palaeolithic (Old Stone Age) and Neolithic (New Stone Age) in 1865, in his *Prehistoric Times*. For him, and for his successors, the Old Stone Age was a time when men used roughly chipped tools; in the New Stone Age they polished them.

Diffusionists and evolutionists

One of the effects of Darwin's theories was that the past was now seen as one line of steady progress from 'Palaeolithic Savagery' to 'Victorian Civilization'. The discovery of the celebrated and developed art of cave paintings from the Stone Age in France somewhat rocked this idea, but it was not until the early twentieth century that it was fairly universally agreed that human cultural evolution had not taken place along a single evolutionary line.

A contemporary of Christian Thomsen, J. J. A. Worsaae, had postulated that ideas must have spread from the region in which they were first formulated. This concept of *diffusionism* gradually gained wide acceptance until late Victorian archaeologists modified it into the idea of 'invasions' to explain how ideas were spread in antiquity. Two rival camps fought battles relentlessly through the last years of the nineteenth century and through a proportion of the twentieth.

The evolutionists, who believed in a single line of human cultural change, were inspired in the late nineteenth century by the anthropologists, Sir Edward Tylor and Lewis Morgan. In 1881 Tylor had suggested that there were three stages in human development, Savagery, Barbarism and Civilization. In *Ancient Society* (1877) Lewis Morgan argued that there were seven such stages, from Lower Savagery to Civilization, the middle stages being designated Barbarism. Lewis Morgan was convinced that new developments did not begin in one place and diffuse outwards. When a society reached a given stage of development, it logically passed on to the next, and the same discoveries could be made in many different parts of the globe at different times. After all, were not explorers of the time demonstrating that civilizations developed quite independently in middle America, without any contact with the Old World?

The diffusionist school of thought was championed most successfully in the twentieth century by Elliot Smith and W. J. Perry. Smith was trained in medicine – he became professor of anatomy at Cairo in 1900, where he became obsessed with the ancient Egyptians. His studies of mummification convinced him that only the Egyptians could have devised such complicated methods of preserving the dead and that therefore, where the practice could be found elsewhere in the world, it must have spread from Egypt. He took his theory further – Egypt was clearly the starting point for all civilization, and to Egypt one must look for the origin of any 'civilized' phenomenon. For him, the chambered tombs of Britain and Europe were clearly derived from Egyptian mastabas. He set out his views in a series of books, such as *The Diffusion of Culture* (1933).

Perry was a more extreme diffusionist. In his *Growth of Civilization* (which reached a wide audience as a Penguin book in 1937) he told how the 'Children of the Sun' set out from Egypt to spread the Heliolithic Civilization across the world. His ideas remained popular. Lord Raglan was a more recent exponent of the view that an invention can only be made once.

However, during the nineteenth century, although the foundations for twentieth-century thought were being laid, the most important task was to recover and arrange data. Excavation techniques were still primitive, and sites were still looted for their antiquities without any regard for the contexts in which they were found. Museums and private collections were stuffed at random with objects and curiosities. The method devised to deal with such diverse material is known as *typology* – the process of arranging artefacts into an evolutionary sequence. It was a typically nineteenth-century solution – based on the idea of unilateral development. It was pioneered in Scandinavia by Oscar Montelius who argued from the pattern of development in railway carriages that objects became more sophisticated and suited to their purpose as time went on. Therefore relative dates could be established from their various stages. In Britain the idea was taken up by Sir John Evans, who applied it to the study of Bronze Age implements, and by William Lane-Fox, better known as General Pitt-Rivers.

General Pitt-Rivers
Augustus Henry Lane-Fox, a professional soldier, had not only developed typology but invented scientific excavation.

4 General A. H. Lane-Fox, better known as General Pitt-Rivers, as he appears in the frontispiece of his privately printed and monumental *Excavations in Cranborne Chase* (1887–98). Pitt-Rivers (1827–1900) was the pioneer of modern field archaeology, meticulously recording all his finds and drawing detailed plans and sections

21

During his military career he had become interested in the development of the rifle and its use, and had been part founder of the Hythe School of Musketry. This stirred his interest in typology, which he utilized to arrange his collection of antiquities. These were eventually displayed in the special annexe of the University Museum in Oxford built for them. In 1880, on condition that he changed his name to Pitt-Rivers, Lane-Fox inherited the 29,000 acres of the Rivers estate in Dorset which included much of Cranborne Chase. Here he had the resources to excavate on his own land, aided by St George Gray, who was responsible for overseeing the actual digging. Pitt-Rivers himself travelled from one site to another (for several were excavated at one time) in a dog cart.

Unlike many of his contemporaries, Pitt-Rivers cared as much for the mundane as the beautiful. 'Common things are more important than particular things', he said, 'because they are more prevalent.' He excavated settlement sites as well as barrows and recorded all his discoveries meticulously, publishing them privately in four sumptuous volumes, *Excavations in Cranborne Chase*. He insisted on total excavation, which he carried out with military precision. Everything, however apparently trivial, was recorded. He set a standard for archaeological excavation that was not bettered until after the First World War.

The twentieth century
By the end of the nineteenth century, then, methods of arranging objects into chronological order through typology, and systems of accurate recording of excavations and of field monuments had been pioneered. The antiquity of Man was established and his evolution from apes was agreed upon. True, not all those interested in the past even attempted to emulate the examples of the pioneers, but knowledge of prehistory was well advanced from the musings of Stukeley. What was required in the early twentieth century was a 'missing link' – an 'apeman'.

The hoax that held back history
In 1912 came the answer to the scholars' prayers. At Piltdown in Sussex a discovery was made of the remains of the famous Piltdown man. The story began in 1908, and the central figure was one Charles Dawson, a Lewes solicitor.

Dawson happened to notice some brown flints while a gravel drive was being built to Barkham Manor, and asked the workmen the source of their material. On tracing it to a quarry nearby, Dawson asked the labourers to report any bones which they encountered. This request was taken at face value, for Dawson was well known as a fossil hunter and antiquary, and in due course, on a subsequent visit, one of the workers produced for him a small fragment of 'brown coconut' which turned out to be a fragmentary left parietal bone of a skull, the rest having been thrown away.

Excited by this discovery, Dawson became a regular visitor to the quarry, scraping away in the hope of finding more bones. His efforts were rewarded. In 1911, by one of those incredible strokes of luck which sometimes occur, he found the fragment of left frontal bone which fitted on to the piece he already possessed, along with other fragments of skull and the premolar of a fossil hippopotamus. Until now Dawson had kept his finds to himself, but now he felt it was time to make them known. He took them along to his old friend in the Natural History Museum, Dr Smith-Woodward, who could hardly believe his eyes. The skull was clearly human, probably the oldest in Britain, if not the world.

In the company of Dawson, Smith-Woodward visited the quarry. Together the two palaeontologists grubbed about in the relatively small hole that was the Piltdown gravel pit. Almost immediately Dawson struck lucky with the discovery of the left-hand portion of a primate jawbone. On successive days subsequently three pieces of cranium were added to the collection. By the end of the summer the haul included eight pieces of what seemed to be human cranium, nine or ten animal teeth and some crude flint implements. In honour of its discoverer Piltdown Man was given the grand name of *Eoanthropus dawsonii* ('Dawson's dawn man') and was presented to the Geological Society at its meeting on 18 December 1912.

The scientific world had learned its lesson about being too sceptical about early human fossils, but they admitted themselves puzzled by the Piltdown remains. The skull looked completely human, while the jawbone resembled that of an ape. Was this the 'apeman' that Darwin had led people to postulate? How old was he? He was certainly the most ancient known man in the world, to judge by the age of the gravels in which he had come to light.

In 1914, in the company of Dawson, the great anthropologist Teilhard de Chardin visited a new site at Piltdown, about 2 miles from the scene of the first discoveries. Here Dawson claimed to have found a molar and isolated fragments of skull among the pebbles raked in clearance to the side of the field. Oddly enough, he had not reported it to Smith-Woodward, apparently keeping it a secret from him

23

for nearly two years and only announcing it when his find was important evidence that Piltdown Man was indeed the missing link.

Dawson died in 1916, secure in the knowledge nearly everyone believed in Piltdown Man. But after his death there were arguments about the age of the mammal fossils found with the Piltdown skull and jaw. Some looked about the right age, but others seemed far too old to be contemporary with Piltdown Man. In 1949 a new technique was being developed for testing the age of fossils, based on the amount of fluorine they had absorbed from the deposit in which they had lain. Dr Kenneth Oakley of the Natural History Museum used the fluorine test to assess the age of the Piltdown bones, and was surprised by the result. Piltdown Man was as young as any of the associated animal fossils, if not very much younger. Indeed, he could not be any older than the Ice Ages, when *Homo sapiens* had already evolved. If he existed, he must have been some kind of freak, certainly not a missing link.

Dr Oakley's tests opened up a new enquiry into Piltdown Man. Dr J. S. Weiner of Oxford University was troubled by the jawbone. It showed certain features in common with that of a chimpanzee, though its teeth had been worn down like a human's. Taking some chimp teeth, he ground them down artificially, and discovered he had made some 'Piltdown' teeth. By 1953 new tests had been developed. Fluorine estimation could provide by now a very close date, and the Piltdown jawbone was quite clearly that of a modern chimpanzee whose teeth had been abraded, their pulp cavities being filled with mineral grains. The cranium fragments were certainly much older, but hardly fossil – estimates put them at about 600 years, not inconceivably the remains of a medieval monk! Jawbone and skull had been stained to match one another. As for the animal fossils, they had come from a variety of sites, by no means all in Britain. The hippopotamus tooth had probably come from Malta, the elephant fossils perhaps from Tunisia. Piltdown Man had been debunked.

Who had perpetrated the hoax? Some have even suggested Teilhard de Chardin was behind it, but that seems unlikely. The most probable candidate is Dawson himself, who has been found associated with another archaeological fraud. Either he was the very gullible victim of a brilliant hoaxer, or he was challenging the arrogance of the academic world. The latter seems more likely. But certainly the result was that important evidence for the origins of Man had been disregarded while Piltdown Man was enjoying his brief but spectacular academic respectability. The disclosure of the hoax proved that the 'missing link' was too simple a concept to have reality – the true line of man's evolution was to be found in the scorching African sun decades later.

The professionals

The First World War brought an end to the traditions of the nineteenth century and ushered in a new era of archae- ology. By 1925 a new generation of archaeologists had emerged, most of them young men with a contempt for the inadequate techniques used by their elders. They were de- termined to put antiquarianism on a professional footing. The inter-war years were among the most tumultuous in archaeological history, and amongst the host of names of those who helped to turn archaeology from the hobby of the rich into an exacting science and a profession, several were outstanding.

Gordon Childe pioneers 'cultures'

Vere Gordon Childe revolutionized the intellectual ap- proach to prehistory. Childe was an Australian, brought up on an intellectual diet of Classics. While a student at Oxford his taste for archaeology was kindled by the study of a type of prehistoric Greek pottery, and from his researches into the pre-Hellenic Greeks he became passionately interested in the prehistoric origins of European society.

Childe was the archetypal absent-minded professor. Conscious of his ugliness, he hid behind a huge handle-bar moustache and a floppy hat, which despite its echoes of Wild Bill Hickok had been made for him by an eminently respectable German hatter. His absent-mindedness was legendary. On one occasion he rolled up his trousers to lead a party of students through the wet grass of the Pentland Hills near Edinburgh, only to forget to unroll them on his return to the city. There he was whisked off by a friend who, seeing the bare legs beneath the long raincoat, imagined him to have forgotten to put on his breeks.

He commonly wore the classic garb of the unworldly don – socks of different colours – and upon occasion unconsciously changed languages as he was speaking. He spoke most European languages and could read all of them. He drove like a madman, sometimes forgetting that he was the driver and once ploughing through a hedge as a result. Once, due to a leaking ceiling, he delivered a lecture from underneath an umbrella. Yet, despite the colour in his personal life, throughout his sixty-five years until his death in Australia in 1957, he poured forth twenty books and dozens of learned

25

papers that set the learned world thinking and re-thinking its ideas about prehistoric Europe.

Undaunted by conflicts, Childe travelled extensively in eastern and central Europe during the turbulent years following the First World War. The outcome was a couple of books which drew together all that was then known about prehistory. Childe believed profoundly that the character of European society was formed by the end of the Neolithic, and he also adhered to the nineteenth-century idea of diffusionism, which he revitalized. He believed that most of the great inventions of mankind originated in the Near East before they spread across Europe and into Asia. He persuaded prehistorians that they should be thinking in economic and social terms rather than in the framework dictated by the technological developments in edge tools. Had Childe been born a century earlier, the terms Stone, Bronze and Iron Ages might never have become popular. For him, the Old Stone Age was distinguished not by the use of roughly chipped stone tools, but by the fact that mankind depended upon hunting and fishing for its livelihood. The New Stone Age for him was not merely a time when stone tools were polished, but one in which Man the Food Gatherer became Man the Food Producer, and was heralded by what he aptly and catchily called the *Neolithic Revolution* (farming)

Above all else Childe gave prehistorians the framework of 'cultures' which he adopted from anthropology. 'Archaeology', he once asserted, 'is the past tense of anthropology.' Childe maintained that a 'culture' was definable by a collection of archaeological remains of distinctive type – diagnostic forms of pots, house plans, flint implements and so on – which taken together were characteristic of a region and period and therefore in archaeological terms represented a 'society' or 'people'. The great limitation of this theory is that when applied to the material remains of historical periods a 'culture' sometimes has no bearing on the politics, language, racial characteristics, etc. of the people. Serious doubt can then be cast on its validity when applied to prehistory. However, as a method of dealing with prehistoric remains it has been seen as viable and thought invaluable.

In 1927 Childe was appointed the first Professor of Prehistoric Archaeology – at Edinburgh University. The chair was founded by Lord Abercromby, traditionally in a fit of pique. He had offered finance for an excavation in Scotland that was to be directed by Pitt-Rivers's right-hand man, St George Gray. His generous offer was turned down by the Society of Antiquaries of Scotland on the grounds that Gray was not a Scot. Abercromby ensured that the first holder of the Edinburgh chair was not a Scot, by specifying, amongst other things, that the incumbent must have first-hand familiarity with Continental material. Only Gordon Childe, the Australian, fitted the job description. From this time on prehistoric archaeology was a respectable subject to study in a British university, and new graduates eventually accelerated the growth of professional archaeology.

Cyril Fox theorizes on the environment

While Childe was persuading prehistorians to think in terms of cultures, a young Cambridge scholar, Cyril Fox, was formulating ideas about the effect of the environment on early man. He tried out his theories in a book which demonstrated that prehistoric patterns of settlement were governed not by modern topography but by patterns of vegetation. This work, *The Archaeology of the Cambridge Region*, appeared in 1923. Following its success, Fox developed his ideas in *The Personality of Britain* (1932), in which he set out his thoughts on geographical determinism. In it he defined the 'Highland' and 'Lowland' zones of Britain – these were to be the geographical model for several generations of archaeologists and historical geographers and the terms are still in use.

Mortimer Wheeler and excavation

Field archaeology did not remain stagnant. Into the trenches vacated by Pitt-Rivers stepped Dr (later Sir) R. E. Mortimer Wheeler. On his return from the Great War he discovered much to challenge him in archaeology. Once more a military man began to conduct excavations with the precision of a martial campaign. By 1920 Wheeler was Keeper of Archaeology in the National Museum of Wales in Cardiff; four years later he had risen to be Director.

He carried out a series of excavations in Wales, mainly on Roman sites, which revived and improved on the methods of Pitt-Rivers. The turning point was reached between 1921 and 1923 during the excavations at Caernarvon, the Roman fort of Segontium. Pitt-Rivers's methods were modified to suit a less splendid and expensive method of publication, but all the rules formulated by the General were followed. For example, drawings were made of the sectioned ground and the stratigraphy was recorded. The coarse pottery received equal attention to the fine, and all the evidence, however trivial, was weighed up and written into a report which owes not a little to the prose of military despatches.

In England in the years up until the Second World War

Wheeler perfected the field techniques he had pioneered in Wales. The names of his excavations are still familiar to scholars fifty years later. At Lydney Park in Gloucestershire he found himself within the confines of an Iron Age fort. At St Albans between 1930 and 1933 he excavated not only inside the Roman city but within the defences of its Iron Age predecessor at Wheathampstead. The climax of Wheeler's career as an excavator in England was reached on a pre-historic site – the vast Iron Age fort of Maiden Castle. This is the largest hill-fort of the period in Britain and had also been a Neolithic sanctuary and a late Roman shrine. Here the Durotriges tribe had made their last desperate stand against the Romans under the leadership of the Emperor-to-be Vespasian in AD 44. And here in 1934 Wheeler not only showed what could be done with a 'big dig' but demon-strated that, far from being the dusty pursuit of antiquaries, archaeology had an immense and immediate popular appeal. On the windswept banks of this prehistoric monument, 'popular archaeology' was born.

Wheeler had for some time been conscious of the archae-ologist's duty to make discoveries known to the general public. He had also realized that popular interest in the subject could have a practical value. Amateur archaeologists were, after all, an invaluable supply of labour and an almost inexhaustible source of funds for further work. Wheeler still had the taste in his mouth of popular acclaim received during his uncovering of the amphitheatre at Caerleon Roman fort in south Wales in 1926. This had been believed to be the original Round Table of King Arthur, and the *Daily Mail* had agreed to finance the 'dig' in return for exclusive reports. Mindful of this experience, Wheeler made pro-vision at Maiden Castle for tourists. He arranged on-site lectures (now a commonplace) and sold literature, postcards and slingstones from the vast cache conveniently left by the Iron Age defenders of the fort. August visitors to the site included Lawrence of Arabia, Sir Arthur Evans (the dis-coverer of Minoan Crete), and Augustus John the painter. Great and humble alike clamoured to scrape for a while in the prehistoric dirt.

Years afterwards, Wheeler wrote:

> When in 1944 I called upon the Viceroy at new Delhi to present my respects, the private secretary who showed me in had worked with us at Maiden Castle. So had an Indian who greeted me at Poona, and another at Calcutta . . . years afterwards in diverse parts of the world, I have come across all manner of people from privates to peers, who had looked over our shoulders or grubbed upon their hands and knees on that hilltop.
> (Wheeler, *Still Digging*, 1958 edn, p. 92.)

O. G. S. Crawford and aerial photography

The Second World War gave archaeologists the new and important tool of aerial photography. Since the sixteenth century antiquaries had realized that sites could often be detected on the ground by crop-marks (the differential growth of vegetation over buried features). The principle behind interpreting crop-marks is very simple; where there are walls or other solid obstructions under the turf, the roots of plants cannot penetrate as deeply and water drains away,

5   The dark circles in the centre of this photograph are the crop-marks of ploughed-out Bronze Age barrows at Cassington, Oxfordshire. The advent of aerial photography this century revolutionized archaeology and led to the discovery of thousands of sites

so they are correspondingly stunted and show up as paler and shorter. Where the earth has been disturbed in the digging of ditches or pits, the roots can penetrate more deeply, minerals and moisture can collect, and the crops are correspondingly higher and greener. From ground level crop-marks can sometimes be detected but their interpretation is usually impossible. From an adjacent hilltop or, ideally, from the air, the pattern etched into the crop growth reflects the plan of buried features. Natural growth of vegetation can thus aid the discovery and planning of otherwise undetectable sites. Nowadays more ancient sites are revealed by aerial photography than by other methods: during the very dry summers of 1976 and 1977, for instance, hundreds of ancient sites came to light from the work of diligent and systematic searchers.

The first archaeological air photographs in Britain were taken in 1906 when a Lieutenant Sharpe took an oblique shot of Stonehenge. The real pioneer of the technique, however, was O. G. S. Crawford. During the Great War he had been an aerial photographer for military purposes and had realized that his skill had archaeological potential. After the war he became the Archaeology Officer for the Ordnance Survey, from which post he was able to develop the new technique. With Alexander Keiller in 1928 he published *Wessex from the Air*.

O. G. S. Crawford had other claims to archaeological fame. Just as Wheeler had followed in the excavational footsteps of Pitt-Rivers, Crawford tramped the tracks of early pioneers of field survey such as J. P. Williams-Freeman, who had been meticulous in recording and planning sites from the visible evidence. It was to Crawford, too, that archaeologists owe one of the most famous publications dealing with the past – *Antiquity*. This was launched in 1927 as a means of bridging the gap between professional and amateur archaeology and has continued in this tradition to the present day.

Hawkes, Piggott and Clark – prehistory untangled

Sir John Evans and Lord Abercromby had their successors. Three young men – Graham Clark, Stuart Piggott and Christopher Hawkes – began studying the artefacts of prehistoric Britain and attacked with vigour the daunting task of arranging them in accordance with the system of cultures developed by Childe.

Graham Clark concentrated on flint tools, and in 1932 introduced prehistorians to a new period, the Mesolithic. This was defined as a period of transition between the Palaeolithic and the Neolithic – when farming had not yet spread to northern Europe but when the Ice Age snows were melting and hunters were following the migrating herds of game.

In the same year Christopher Hawkes, then working in the British Museum, collaborated with his senior colleague Sir Thomas Kendrick on a national survey of British archaeology, *Archaeology in England and Wales, 1914–31*, which became the basic text-book for British prehistorians for years thereafter. Hawkes was mostly concerned with the Iron Age and the problems of classifying its pottery, though he had also given careful consideration to the Bronze Age.

This left the Neolithic for Stuart Piggott who, also in the same year, brought out his survey of *Neolithic Pottery of the British Isles*. It was indeed a stirring twelve months for pre-

history, since it too saw the publication of Fox's *Personality of*
Britain (p. 27).

Cambridge became the centre for British prehistoric research in the mid-1930s and it was in this foremost university town that the first society dedicated to research on the period – the Prehistoric Society – was founded in 1935.

Thus on the eve of the Second World War prehistoric archaeology might have seemed destined for a period of dynamic development. Many archaeologists were amongst those who, alas, did not return from the war, and the survivors inevitably had to postpone their research into the past. However, the end of the war saw Wheeler, Piggott and the then unknown Glyn Daniel and T. G. E. Powell in India. Piggott and Daniel were actively engaged in interpreting aerial photographs and Piggott was devoting much attention to untangling Indian prehistory. Wheeler was appointed Director General of Archaeology in the sub-continent, and, except for an excavation at Stanwick in Yorkshire in 1951–2, his contribution to archaeology lay mainly outside Britain, though his British television popularity was yet to come.

After the war, archaeology not surprisingly took some time to gain momentum again, but the late 1940s saw some important innovations, not the least of which was the discovery of radio-carbon dating in 1946.

Science and archaeology

If any single discovery can be claimed to have revolutionized prehistoric archaeology it was this method of dating discovered in 1946 by W. F. Libby. The essence of Libby's discovery was that the radioactive isotope of carbon, known as Carbon^{14} is absorbed by all living organisms during their lifetime. On the death of the organism it starts to decay at a fixed rate. After 5730 years it is half as radioactive as it was when the organism died. This period is known as the half-life, after which the decay of radioactivity is too irregular to be reliably measurable.

Overnight the problem of dating the prehistoric past moved from inspired guesswork and logical deduction to a realm where relative dates could be used. Up to this time dates had been calculated by a long chain of links and associations from the historical civilizations of the Near East and eastern Mediterranean. To a greater or lesser extent these areas were 'historical' from around 3000 BC, but before that there were no clues to either real or relative chronology. Perhaps the most amazing feature of the 'radio-carbon revolution' was the extent to which the dates assigned by prehistorians to particular cultures were correct. Even for a period as remote as the Neolithic in Britain the experts had been right to assign, for instance, the appearance of copper metallurgy to soon after 2000 BC. They had, however, allowed a mere 500 years for the period as a whole, which radio-carbon proved to be too short a time. Sadly this method of dating was indeed too good to be true, and it was discovered to have serious drawbacks. It is not now regarded as infallible since it is demonstrably inaccurate in many circumstances. The system of dating used in this book is explained in the Appendix, pp. 191.

It is very probable that the sudden increase in the use of 'science' for archaeological purposes in the late 1940s and early 1950s was due to the acceleration of research for military reasons during the war. For example, 1946 saw Richard Atkinson using electrical prospecting for investigating the Neolithic and Bronze Age complex of Dorchester-on-Thames. In 1948 fluoride testing was first applied to fossil bones, a technique which later led to the uncovering of the Piltdown forgery (p. 22).

The growth of popular archaeology

The social changes brought about by the First World War led to alterations in the ranks of amateur archaeology. From this time on people from all walks of life began to show an interest. Their fascination with the past was secured by the publicity that accompanied the discovery of the tomb of Tutankhamun in Egypt and by that enjoyed by Wheeler's excavations. The new amateur archaeologists were in many respects a more active breed than their predecessors: often they were city dwellers, anxious to 'get away from it all' to a country idyll where they could observe field monuments. Their tastes generally ran to more strenuous pursuits than listening to improving lectures by antiquaries or attending sedate picnics at ruined abbeys.

Flint hunting was an all-consuming passion of many. Armed with knee-protectors cut from the tyres of the increasingly popular motor-car (itself a stimulus to rural pursuits), amateur antiquaries crawled indomitably across ploughed fields collecting treasures with which they enriched many a local museum. Local activities flourished, catered for by a spate of 'Field Clubs' rather than antiquarian societies. Literature began to encourage archaeological tourism – books such as Weigall's *Wanderings in Roman Britain*. On a less practical level, popular education led to an influx of manuals which explained 'how people lived' in the past. One such, by Gordon Childe, was entitled with staggering comprehensiveness *What Happened in History*

(1942). Another example was the *Everyday Life* series by Marjorie and C. H. B. Quennell. Although in some respects out of date even in the 1920s, these books helped to foster interest in a more remote past than was embraced by school curricula.

The 1950s saw further advances in the development of popular archaeology. On Saturday 18 September 1954 a marble head of the god Mithras came to light on the Roman site of the Walbrook in London. The following day its picture was reproduced in the *Sunday Times*. The site was opened to visitors during weekday evenings. 'No one knew what to expect,' wrote the excavator Professor W. F. Grimes later, 'perhaps 500 people, it was thought. The police estimated the queue that wound round the streets was at least five times that figure.' The queue continued and by the end of the week visitors were demanding floodlights and other facilities. The discovery had caught the popular imagination. The excavator explained, 'The climax of these nocturnal happenings came on Sunday 26 September, when literally in the dark and photographed by flashlight the head of a deity, not then recognized as Minerva, was found. It was removed from the ground by my assistant (as she was then) and displayed to the still waiting crowds outside by Norman Cook as he conveyed it to the safe custody of the Guildhall Museum. A banner headline in the local paper "back home" dealt ambiguously with this event. "WELSH WOMAN" it said "FINDS GOD".' (W. F. Grimes, *Excavation of Roman and Medieval London* (1968), p. 232.)

The publicity given to the Mithraic Temple reflected only a fraction of the popular enthusiasm at the time. There is no doubt that at this period archaeologists existed who managed to be everything that the public wanted them to be – erudite, witty, slightly eccentric, but nevertheless able to put across their subject in an intelligible and entertaining manner.

In 1952–3 vast numbers of families bought television sets in order to watch the Coronation of Queen Elizabeth II. The cult of television personalities was relatively new, and archaeology and the television made a popular marriage during the next decade. Televisions were mostly to be found in the more prosperous homes, where the viewers demanded that the people entertaining them seemed to be at least their social equals. Mortimer Wheeler (who was knighted at this period mainly for having presented archaeology to the people through his television appearances) was an ideal candidate for a television personality at the time. He was of distinguished appearance, with wavy hair, military moustache and upright bearing. He sounded distinguished with an 'Oxford' accent (though in fact he studied at London), and he was witty, urbane and profoundly knowledgeable.

Wheeler's meteoric rise to 'Television Personality of the Year' was affected through the agency of the highly popular parlour game, *Animal, Vegetable, Mineral?* The quiz chairman, Glyn Daniel (now professor of prehistoric archaeology at Cambridge), put before the team various objects which had been sent by challenging museums, and awarded marks for the answers given. The team members varied, but included such familiar prehistorians as Childe and Piggott, the art historian Thomas Bodkin and various less flamboyant figures. Wheeler was invariably the star of the show, making up with witticisms where his knowledge failed him. Throughout Britain there must be thousands of people, including one of the present authors, whose curiosity in the past was fanned by the programme.

The inventor of *Animal, Vegetable, Mineral?* was the brilliant producer Paul Johnstone. He was responsible for an imaginative series of documentaries entitled *Buried Treasure*, which were the forerunners of the modern programme *Chronicle* which he also devised. Practical experiments were carried out on the screen to determine, for instance, how many men were needed to haul the stones of Stonehenge, or whether it were possible to transport the boulders the distances postulated. Thanks to the inspiration of *Buried Treasure* stalwart scholars and enthusiasts tried to build prehistoric houses and to live in the discomfort of the Neolithic village of Skara Brae in which the original stone furniture survives. People valiantly attempted to blow Bronze Age horns, courageously ate Iron Age meals and nattily sported Bronze Age clothes. Children's interests in the past were catered for by *Treasure Hunt*.

The fever of archaeology was reflected too in radio where the pioneer was the writer Leonard Cottrell, who produced some of the best popular books on the subject. Other writers were highly successful with subjects ranging from the British prehistoric period to the ancient civilizations of the Mediterranean.

The end of the 1950s marked a waning in interest – several of the personalities had died and anthropology and zoology replaced archaeology in popularity on television. The interest in the past was not taken up again by the media until around 1967 when once more 'big digs' began to hit the headlines. In the interval, a new type of popular archaeology had emerged. Each year young people between the ages of about 18 and 24 flocked to take part in excavations. They were not, as a rule, more than superficially attracted to the archaeological aspect of the activity, but it is probable that their reasons were similar to those that sent their fellows into kibbutzim or communes. The stimulus for this 'drop-out' archaeology was almost certainly the excavation at Masada in Israel, a citadel of the Zealots. Under the direction of professor Yigael Yadin, it was announced that anyone would be welcome as a volunteer digger, with no questions asked about their motives or identity. Young people from all over Europe travelled to join the team hoping no doubt, like their kindred spirits the 'flower children', to find enlightenment. Not all could go to Masada, but there were other digs nearer home. In Britain the large-scale excavations at Winchester that started in 1962, for instance, rose to popularity. In 1966 a rival attraction for romantic youth was provided in the investigations into the Iron Age hill-fort at South Cadbury, Somerset, by Leslie Alcock (now professor of archaeology at Glasgow). This had earlier occupation and has also been identified with the Camelot of the legendary and semi-historical King Arthur.

Since the late 1960s, however, the media have in general been reluctant to sponsor any large-scale archaeological projects, and money from other sources has for general economic reasons been unavailable. The media has perhaps been more confident of attracting audiences with occultism than with prehistory proper. The interest in the occult aspect of the past casts interesting reflections on why people are interested in archaeology at all. The 1970s have seen a boom in books on 'ancient mysteries' which began with such works as Erich von Däniken's *Chariot of the Gods* and T. C. Lethbridge's *The Legend of the Sons of God*. Lethbridge was an archaeologist who became obsessed with the occult powers of standing stones and similar monuments. Like many after him, he believed in the lost powers of ancient peoples, and in the ability of standing stones to contain energy. The idea was not novel – it had been set out in the 1920s by Alfred Watkins in *The Old Straight Track*. Lethbridge also put forward the suggestion, developed independently by von Däniken, that men from outer space may have had a hand in the works of prehistoric man. The popularity of these ideas is easy to understand, although most have been disproved by more scientific research; the romance of the past and the mystery of prehistory have been linked with the second area of mystery and romance in the modern world – outer space.

The new age archaeology

As we have seen, the full value of 'science' to the archaeologist was not realized until the 1950s and was concurrent with the growth of popularity in the subject. Four main areas were affected. First, dating was made easier by the discovery of the radio-carbon method (above) and by the use of potassium argon. The latter method depended on the gradual conversion of potassium to argon gas inside volcanic rocks and had important implications for the dating of the earliest hominid fossils found in Africa. Other techniques of finding chronological hangers for the past now include thermoluminescence (based on the measurement of light emitted by minerals trapped in pottery at the time of firing, which have absorbed radiation), and the study of archaeomagnetism or remnant magnetic dating (which stems from a study of the changes in axis of the earth's magnetic pole). A method that involves tree-rings (dendrochronology) was pioneered at the start of this century and had repercussions eventually since it showed that radio-carbon dating was not always accurate.

Second, science played a part in the detection of sites. Not only has aerial photography revolutionized the study, but such techniques as resistivity monitoring and, more recently, methods of measuring magnetism have become invaluable.

Third, science has aided the analysis of materials. While the first antiquarians were forced to rely on guesswork, it is now possible to make accurate analyses of such objects as Neolithic stone axes. It is common nowadays to be able to pinpoint the place of manufacture or origin of almost any geological specimen. Metals too can be analysed to detect trace elements and possible sources of the raw material, as well as to determine the techniques of manufacture. Organic remains have been put under the microscope and the flotation of carbonized plant material from excavation, for example, has led to a greater understanding of ancient landscape.

Fourth, the mathematical analysis of finds has recently enjoyed a popularity amongst archaeologists. Statistical methods have been employed by prehistorians wishing to classify flint tools, and these methods have been extended to pottery. In 1962 a young Cambridge scholar, Dr David Clark, published a study of matrix analysis as applied to British Beaker pottery, a famous type of late Neolithic ceramic. In it Clark suggested that the intuitive methods of studying finds previously employed by prehistorians were too imprecise; instead of inspired guesswork based on logical deductions, their calculations should be based on statistical evidence. It is probably too early to assess the impact of this upon archaeological studies, but there is no doubt that it has had a profound short-term effect.

The development of scientific techniques has played an important part in the growth of what is termed New Archaeology. Because of the greater variety of material and its retrieval and analysis it has been possible to observe the past from a sociological point of view. Where the retrieval of data is still impossible, instead of giving in to romantic fantasies like the first antiquarians, modern archaeologists have sometimes turned to modern societies which are in the same stages of development as those in the past. Thus in seeking the motives of those who built Stonehenge, some scholars have travelled to Easter Island and questioned why the natives there erected huge stone heads. This approach to prehistory has mainly been used in North America where the archaeological evidence is sparse and where prehistoric studies are still closely connected with anthropology.

Trends in studying the past, and in particular the prehistoric past, are always a reflection of the intellectual climate of the day and it is interesting to compare the various interpretations put on one monument throughout the ages. These have often less connection with which techniques of study were available, than with the overriding questions of the day. Take, for instance, Stonehenge, a prehistoric monument which has at all times been central to thinking on the British past. To medieval monks it was the work of Merlin, a part of Arthurian Romance. With the revival of interest in things Classical during the Renaissance it was seen as a Roman temple, even though there is no mention of it in any Roman literature. In the eighteenth century the romanticism of William Stukeley turned it into a druid temple, and so it remained until Victorian times. Although throughout the twentieth century it has remained firmly prehistoric, the aspects of Stonehenge that have been found most fascinating are those which echo trends in contemporary science. In the 1920s people were asking how it was built. In the 1930s they demanded to know the source of the stones, geological studies having recently shown that it was possible to identify the provenance of rocks. The 1940s and early 1950s were the period in which Childe's model of cultures was at the forefront of prehistorians' minds, and accordingly they asked, 'What culture was responsible for the erection of Stonehenge?' At this point, too, scholars were under the spell of Childe's ideas of modified diffusionism and felt it necessary to evoke Mycenaean connections to explain the achievement of the builders. The

37

mid-1950s saw the first Sputnik and the beginnings of space exploration. Accordingly men saw Stonehenge in terms of some kind of prehistoric observatory. The computer revolutions of the 1960s led to Stonehenge being seen as a type of early computer, set up by prehistoric mathematical Einsteins. The 1970s have been host to two approaches to the monument. Some people, preoccupied with the occult, have connected it with prehistoric understanding of mysterious earth forces. Others, more down-to-earth, have taken the sociological view and asked, 'What kind of society put this up? How were the builders organized?' Each time, depending on the questions asked it, Stonehenge has given up its answers. Like the Delphic oracle, its meanings have to be interpreted by its latter-day priests, and their interpretations tell us perhaps more about the priests and the suppliants than about Stonehenge itself.

Current thinking on human origins

In the 1870s the great antiquity of Man and his evolution from a more primitive primate was recognized, though at times hotly disputed. However, the debates took on further refinements; the knotty problem of how to define a man, and therefore the exact age of the human race, took on a significance. Which of the many 'man-like' fossils should be regarded as the remains of the earliest men? Even today there is a tendency to wish to put an exact date to the precise moment when a weird ape-like creature pushed himself to his feet with hairy, paw-like hands and stutteringly cried aloud, 'I am *Homo sapiens*!' It is as difficult to define a human being as it is to define death. A human must speak, stand erect and make tools, for example. But what happens when some but not all the requirements are present? The battles over fragments of bone are fierce. The remains are sparse as well as ambiguous. Because man evolved before many rocks were laid down, the fossil remains are necessarily difficult to find. In one of the areas where fossils have been discovered in substantial numbers (Olduvai Gorge) the problems are exacerbated by the fact that the rocks, although of immense antiquity, are extremely powdery. Finds cannot therefore be indisputably proved to have been embedded in a matrix of a particular date – it can merely be recorded that they were associated with rocks of a particular date. It is thus not surprising that the question of the origin of man is surrounded by fierce debates even today.

The age of the earth itself and the methods by which this time is fixed are of vital importance in the search for man's oldest ancestor. Scholars are dealing with periods so remote that radio-carbon, bristlecone pine and many other scientific methods of dating are irrelevant and useless. These methods deal in thousands of years and cannot be applied when dealing with millions. Within the hundred or so years in which it has been recognized that man evolved, it has become necessary to juggle geological facts and data with the fossil remains of man to arrive at a picture of the past. The prehistoric past of man is given dramatic interest not by the royal murders or internecine wars of the historical period, but by the Ice Ages and inventions that today the world takes for granted. Perhaps the most astounding aspect of the prehistoric past is still that which the Victorians had difficulty in grasping – namely that Man is extremely old. It took roughly 3 million years for the first standing, conversing man to think of living in a town, and a mere 10,000 to progress from that state to one where he walked on the moon.

Man and the geological past

The world is now thought to be 4,600,000,000 years old, a time-span which has been divided into eras composed of periods. For the purpose of tracing the antiquity of man it is only the last era that is of importance – the Cenozoic. Of the seven periods into which this is divided only the Miocene, Pliocene, Pleistocene and Holocene were probably peopled with hominids. The last two are commonly grouped together and termed the Quaternary. The Pleistocene is distinguished by being the period of the great Ice Ages and is of special relevance in British prehistoric development, since it was not until one of the warmer periods within the Ice Ages that the first men appeared in Britain – well after the main developments in man's evolution had taken place.

The Pleistocene began between $3\frac{1}{2}$ and $2\frac{1}{2}$ million years ago and during the period there were several warm *inter-glacials* which alternated with cold *glacials*. These stretches of time are known by different names in Britain and on the Continent, and each was of importance to man since he was unable to improve his environment but had to adapt to each change. During certain uncongenial periods, for instance, there were no men in Britain.

The Pleistocene is to be roughly equated with the archaeologist's term Palaeolithic – the Old Stone Age. This is the classic period of popular caveman mythology when the climate was harsh and standards of living unbelievably hard to modern minds. Geology and archaeology are very closely connected at this period and the chronological divisions – upper, middle and lower Palaeolithic – refer to the levels of the deposits in which the archaeological material was found. The upper Palaeolithic is thus the most recent of the three.

The early antiquarians were wrong not only in their estimation of the age of Man but also in the areas in which they searched – the chief developments were enacted outside Britain. The development of monkey-like creatures began before the process of Continental Drift had led to the separation of Europe and Africa from North and South America. Remains of a monkey-like creature found at Purgatory Hill, Montana, have been taken as proof – but the climate became too cold to support primate life and the species died out, leaving the development of primates to take place in the warmer and more densely vegetated areas of Europe and Asia. Until this period, about 12 million years ago, Europe, India, East Africa and Arabia had been cloaked in dense forest, but cooler weather led to the gradual replacement of this by open grasslands, over a period of about 10 million years until the onset of the Ice Age.

However, the primates in these areas were still able to support themselves in health. Today the term 'primate' covers two main sub-orders – the prosimians (mouse, lemur, tarsier) and the apes and monkeys. The apes include chimpanzees and Man. All seem to have been developed from a common ancestor – a rat-like creature who, about 70 million years ago, learned to abstain from eating insects in favour of a diet of leaves. Accordingly it took to living in

Table 1 Human evolution

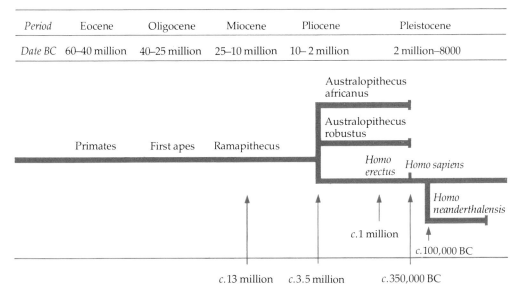

Period	Eocene	Oligocene	Miocene	Pliocene	Pleistocene
Date BC	60–40 million	40–25 million	25–10 million	10–2 million	2 million–8000

trees and within 15 million years the line that became apes and monkeys diverged from the prosimians.

Most recent evidence and scholarly thought has led to the conclusions that *Homo erectus* had become the major species of hominid by 1.5 million years ago. He was important to the development of modern man because his adventurous spirit gave impetus to the movement of his kind to areas outside Africa where they had evolved. With a boldness comparable to that shown by modern space explorers, *Homo erectus* literally went 'where no man had been before'. He and his fellows simply walked out of Africa across the convenient strip of land that connected it to Asia.

His people reached China where remains have been found in a cave at Choukoutien. Here the *Homo erectus* colonists are referred to as Pekin Man. They may have had more desirable characteristics, but amongst their other activities they certainly practised cannibalism and had discovered fire. A clear if short scenario of life at Choukoutien can be sketched from the remains of about 35 adults and 10 children found there. In the cave they warmed themselves around a fire – a simple comfort it might seem, except that

6 Partly restored skull of a *Homo erectus* individual. Although no actual remains of *Homo erectus* have been found in Britain, it is likely that this hominid was responsible for some of the flint tools found here. *Homo erectus* was the forerunner of modern man (*Homo sapiens*) – he had a heavier jaw and more pronounced brow ridge

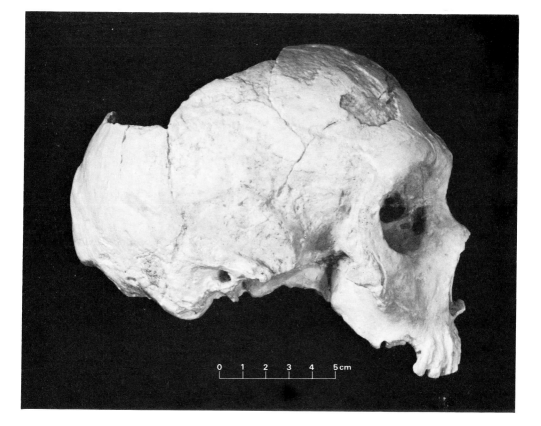

0 1 2 3 4 5 cm

this was the first time that any man is known to have used flame. They had all the modern conveniences of the time, for they used chopper tools in their everyday life. It all seems a far cry from the Creation of Adam on 23 October 4004 BC.

Homo erectus did not confine his activity to China but moved south in the Orient to Java where he is known as Java Man, and others of the species led their families to the greener pastures of Europe. The type found in one part of Germany, for instance, is known as Heidelberg Man.

The oldest *Homo erectus* skull found in Africa, to date, was one unearthed in East Turkana in 1975. It compares closely with the other *Homo erectus* fossils, and has a skull capacity of about 900cc. Considerable variety is shown in the capacities of *Homo erectus* skulls which range from 775cc to 1300cc, compared with 1400cc in modern humans. From such remains we can tell that these early explorers had broad, flat noses, backward-sloping chins, projecting faces and a pointed back to their skulls.

Such were the 'human' inhabitants of the globe half a million years ago when Europe was caught up in the Ice Ages. In Europe *Homo erectus* conservatively used hand-axes as he always had done, and even the most up-to-date *Homo* still used the chopper tools evolved by his ancestors. Human development was ripe for another step forward. Into the void shuffled *Homo sapiens*. As far as can be ascertained at this remove, this hominid directly developed from *Homo erectus* and various types are distinguished, for instance, *Homo sapiens* (unspecialized), *Homo sapiens sapiens* (modern man), and the most famous archetypal caveman, *Homo sapiens neanderthalensis*. This fascinating variation of man was the first hominid to show evidence of any character in the modern sense. With his heavy brow ridges and thick jaw, retreating forehead and massive limbs, he has become a celebrated personality of prehistory. His brain capacity was in excess of that of some modern men and there is evidence of his social feelings and personal ties. Classic Neanderthals died out for reasons that are unclear, but not (in the light of recent research) without bequeathing at least some blood to the early *Homo sapiens*.

Homo sapiens sapiens was not simply one type – one of the earliest variations was Cro-Magnon Man, who appears to have been dominant in upper Palaeolithic Europe. Where Neanderthal Man had been content to hunt for his food with few weapons, Cro-Magnon Man used a variety of spears, harpoons and arrows. He learned to fish with a range of tackle, and to produce a variety of bone and antler tools. His flint working was superior. He devised a type of steep retouch for shaping points, which concentrated on the strongest part of the blade and provided a blunt back for the finger to rest on or to prevent the cords being frayed when the flints were mounted in hafts. He invented a variety of blades and burins for the cuttings of antler and bone. Last, but not least, he discovered art.

Chapter two

The explorers – Man challenges the environment (Palaeolithic and Mesolithic)

On the track of Palaeolithic Man

Icy cold, damp and dark, Wookey Hole is a likely place in which the imaginative can conjure up nameless horrors from the dawn of time. The Wookey Hole ravine is sliced into the Mendip Hills of Somerset. At one end, from a rock face, cascades the river Axe, liberated from the underground tunnels it has cut through the limestone in the past millennia. On one side of the gorge is a rustic bridge that would have delighted any Victorian lady. It leads to a cave known dramatically as the Hyena Den. This cavern of modest proportions was investigated in the nineteenth century by the indefatigable cave explorer Sir William Boyd Dawkins. Its floor was found to be littered with the fragmentary remains of the meals enjoyed by generation after generation of hyenas. Cave lion, cave bear, grizzly bear, mammoth, woolly rhinoceros, bison and Irish elk were also represented. And in the midst of these remains were the hearths and tools of some of the early human occupants of the British Isles. Life could not have been particularly pleasant for these intrepid hunters, and the cave is not of spectacular interest by itself, but it is one of the very few places in Britain that is known to have been the home of Palaeolithic Man.

The sources

The remains of the British Palaeolithic fall into the same three main divisions that can be observed on the Continent. In the lower Palaeolithic, which coincided with a warm period during the Ice Age, men's handiwork mostly took the form of what are known as core-tools – axes and choppers produced by chipping pieces off a lump of flint. Two main traditions can be distinguished in Britain. The earliest is called Clactonian after Clacton-on-Sea in Essex where it was first recognized, and is an industry characterized by crude choppers and more especially by tools made from the flakes detached from them, and the later is called the Acheulian after a site in France. This is typified by superior chipped axes of various forms.

With the onset of a colder period the middle Palaeolithic is distinguishable. The remains of this period are very sparse in Britain and consist of new types of axes and flake tools made by a complicated technique which involved preparing the core first before the finished tool was detached. This was the golden age of Neanderthal Man on the Continent, and the presence in Britain of tools of the type used by Neanderthalers (Mousterian tools) suggests that some of these men as well as their implements crossed the land-bridge from France.

The upper Palaeolithic coincided with the last great Ice Age. This was the period of the cave dwellers, and the time in which *Homo sapiens sapiens* established his supremacy. The tools of this time are fashioned out of flakes rather than cores (i.e. they are blade industries), and are much more neatly finished off than previously. From this period some bone tools have been discovered, and also the earliest examples of art in Britain.

In around 12,000 BC the ice began to melt and the climate improved. This early post-glacial period is known archaeologically as the Mesolithic (middle Stone Age) and marks the adaptation of the upper Palaeolithic societies to the changing environment. Men followed the rapidly migrating herds of animals, and spread out through the forests that gradually covered much of Britain. The flintwork of the Mesolithic comprises mainly 'microliths', very small tools, often geometric in shape, that were mounted up to form composite blades. Some axes and other tools are also found among the forest dwellers. A few bone and antler tools belong to this period, notably harpoons. Some 'settlements' are known, of which the richest is Star Carr in Yorkshire. Homes appear to have been insubstantial windbreaks and art is absent in Britain.

Tool-making
To the uninitiated, flint tools usually look identical to their naturally produced brothers. Since tools are such vital evidence in chronicling Stone Age man, it is worth while considering how they are recognized.

It is true that naturally flaked flints can look uncommonly like man-made implements, but there are certain tell-tale differences. If a man is flaking a flint, he will probably use a stone as a hammer, or a bone or a stick as a 'fabricator'. He will direct his blows so that chips are removed where he wants to detach them, so first, a man-made tool is likely to show a series of flakes which are all detached from the same angle. If a stone or other tool is used the flake detached will have certain characteristics too. One such is a pronounced 'striking platform', on which the blow was aimed. At the point at which the hammerstone fell there will be a 'bulb of percussion', radiating out from which will be tiny cracks or 'fissures'. Below the bulb of percussion a secondary flake scar will be observable, the 'bulbar scar'. From the bulb of percussion the fracture will radiate like waves. Usually, if a

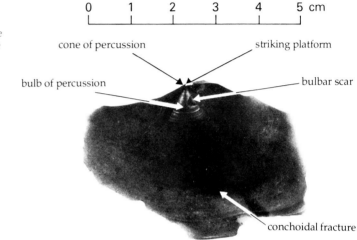

7 Flint flake from the neolithic axe factory at Grimes Graves, Norfolk, showing the features of a man-struck flake

flake has been detached by human agency, there will be signs of 'secondary flaking' along the edge, where it has been 'sharpened' to cut. This may vary from fairly coarse to fine. Sometimes it may have a rippled effect – 'ripple flaking'. If a stone hammer has been used, these features will be very pronounced. If a softer tool was used they will be much less discernible.

While naturally chipped flints may show many of these features, there are usually certain differences. For instance, flakes will have been detached from random angles. If frost has resulted in flaking, it will have produced distinct flake scars which are noticeably without a conchoidal fracture – there may be shallow rings but no clear ripples, and they will be concentric, producing what is termed a 'pot lid' fracture. Thermal fractures never have bulbs of percussion or bulbar scars. Occasionally frost produced a 'starch' fracture – the flint will look like a column or rod, with parallel flakes detached from it. Once again, however, there will be no apparent striking platform, bulb of percussion or bulbar scar, and the conchoidal ripples will be faint.

If flint implements have been transported by water or ice,

they will have become abraded or 'rolled'. This can be a helpful clue when flint implements have been carried a long way from their place of origin.

Flint tools are often 'patinated'. The commonest type of patina is the all-over white 'skin' on flints which have been lying on chalk. This is due to contact with minerals, and takes a long time to form. It can be used, in conjunction with other evidence, to prove whether a flint is a modern 'forgery', since it cannot be produced artificially. Outside the chalk areas, other kinds of patina can form – red, brown, ochre, yellow and even green. Sometimes patinas are distinctive of particular regions, and can be used to determine the origins of a tool even if the details of the findspot are lost.

Men arrive in Britain – the lower Palaeolithic

There is very little evidence to dispute that men arrived in Britain relatively late in human development. No fossils of the first men have come to light at all, and the tools which are unequivocally the work of humans and securely datable are not much older than a quarter of a million years. Earlier tools have been claimed to exist but they are all the subject of controversy and debate.

The oldest tools to have been claimed as the work of 'ancient Britons' may not be tools at all. They were once known picturesquely as 'Dawn Tools' (or eoliths), and have sometimes been named 'rostro-carinates' due to their shape. But were they human handiwork? Most are so crude that it is impossible to be certain and natural causes may be called in to explain their tool-like shape. Others are undoubtedly tools. But were they genuinely associated with the geological deposits in which they were supposedly found? They could be hoaxes, or may have found their way into the ancient strata by accident when the ground was disturbed.

Take, for instance, the case of finds from the Red Crag at Foxhall, Norfolk. The East Anglian Crags are central to the debate on eoliths for they have a disconcerting habit of yielding tool-like flints to discerning collectors. A number of eoliths were found at Foxhall, supposedly associated with a human jaw. There is little doubt that the Foxhall flints are genuine tools, but . . . there are two important buts. The human jaw is almost certainly recent, and the tools are flake not core implements. If they have genuinely come from Red Crag, they must be at least a million years old. But a million years ago not only were there no examples of *Homo sapiens* around in Britain, but there were no examples of flake tools either.

Then there is the perplexing case of the Sidestrand axe from Norfolk. It is undoubtedly an axe, but of what date? Its context suggests that fairly advanced axes were being chipped in Norfolk between three and four million years ago. If that were true, Africa would have to look to its laurels as the Garden of Eden, and a great many Victorian antiquaries would be vindicated. The Sidestrand object is an

Table 2 Palaeolithic and Mesolithic

Date	Period	Environment	Man	
c.750,000 – c.350,000 BC	Cromerian interglacial	Warm Birch, pine, spruce Bison, horse, hippo, rhino, mammoth		Westbury-sub-Mendip Very early Acheulian?
c.350,000 – c.250,000 BC	Anglian glacial	Cold Grasses and sedges		Acheulian (Kent's Cavern) Fordwich
c.250,000 – c.200,000 BC	Hoxnian interglacial	Warm Birch, pine, oak, alder Hippo, rhino, cave bear, cave lion, horse		Clactonian Acheulian *Homo erectus?* *Homo sapiens*
c.200,000 – c.125,000 BC	Wolstonian glacial	Cold Grasses and sedges Woolly rhino, wolf, reindeer, cave lion		Clactonian (dies out) Acheulian Levallois *Homo sapiens*
c.125,000 – c.70,000 BC	Ipswichian interglacial	Warm Birch, pine Hippopotamus, hyena, bison, aurochs, red deer, cave lion		Acheulian? Levallois Mousterian *Homo neanderthalensis?* *Homo sapiens*
c.70,000 – c.8000 BC	Devensian glacial (For details, see Table 3)	Cold Grasses and sedges Mammoth, woolly rhino, reindeer, musk ox, horse, lemming	Lower Palaeolithic Middle Palaeolithic Upper Palaeolithic	{Acheulian? {Levallois? Mousterian {'Proto-Solutrean' {'Aurignacian' {Creswellian {'Cheddarian' *Homo neanderthalensis* *Homo sapiens*
c.8300 BC to date	Post-glacial or Flandrian	Warm	Mesolithic hunters and gatherers	{Maglemosian {Obanian {Geometric {microliths

 Ice Ages

odd sort of axe for any period. It has understandably been dismissed as a Neolithic rough-out of about 3000 BC that has found its way into an ancient deposit by accident; a much more comfortable theory than one which would turn the learned journals upside down.

A few tools have been found at Fordwich, Kent, and Kent's Cavern near Torquay, which many experts believe belong to a warm spell in the 'Anglian' glaciation, perhaps 350,000 years ago. These are very crude hand-axes which can be compared with rough tools of the same period in

Table 3 Palaeolithic and Mesolithic: last (Devensian) glacial and post-glacial

Date	Period	Environment	Man	
c.70,000 – c.59,000 BC	Early glacial	Sub-arctic tundra		Britain uninhabited?
c.59,000 – c.54,000 BC	Chelford interstadial	Northern coniferous forest		Acheulian? Levallois?
c.54,000 – c.40,000 BC	Mid-glacial	Sub-arctic tundra		Britain uninhabited?
c.40,000 – c.28,000 BC	Interstadial (Upton Warren, etc.)	Temperate – open grassy plains		Mousterian culture Neanderthal Man
c.28,000 – c.23,000 BC	Mid-glacial	Cold, open – juniper, willow, pine, birch		Early upper Palaeolithic tools
c.23,000 – c.12,000 BC	Full glacial	Formation of ice sheets		Britain uninhabited
c.12,000 – c.8300 BC	Late glacial	Park tundra (Pollen Zone I, sub-arctic) (Pollen Zone II, Allerød, warmer interstadial) (Pollen Zone III, sub-arctic)		Creswellian 'Cheddarian' (i.e. late upper Palaeolithic tools)
c.8300 BC to date	Post-glacial or Flandrian	Pollen Zone IV Pre-boreal, c.8300– 7500 BC, warmer Pollen Zone V, VI Boreal, c.7500– 5500 BC, increasing warmth Pollen Zone VIIa Atlantic, c.5500– 3200 BC, climatic optimum	Mesolithic	⎧ Maglemosians ⎪ Blade and trapeze ⎨ industries ⎪ Obanian, etc. ⎩ ———————— Neolithic colonists

Very cold conditions

France. The similarities might be regarded as fortuitous but in Kent's Cavern they were found with the bones of creatures that scientists believe were extinct by the start of the next warm period, when it is known that man was likely to have been present in Britain.

The oldest wooden implement in the world

With the warmer period that geologists have termed the Hoxnian interglacial we leave the quicksands of debate on eoliths to enter a world in which bands of hunters undoubtedly roamed Britain.

The earliest traces of man in Britain about which there is real certainty have come to light at Clacton-on-Sea, Essex, where now holidaymakers relax in the holiday camp and play golf on the nearby course, with the vestiges of some of the first people in Britain beneath their feet. The Clacton site was first investigated in the early part of this century, but in 1969–70 more extensive excavations were carried out on the golf course.

The main tools found at Clacton are 'choppers' in the same general tradition as examples found for instance at Vértes-szöllös in Hungary. To judge from these finds, the people who hunted at Clacton were members of *Homo sapiens*, but the absence of any bone fossils leaves this in the realm of speculation.

At the time the Clacton tool-makers were inhabiting the site, the North Sea had not formed. Instead, they were living on the edge of a long-vanished stream, where the gravelly bank provided a good place, free from mud, to obtain water. The climate they enjoyed seems to have been fairly clement, and there was an abundant supply of bison, fallow deer, rhino and elephant to provide food and the spice of danger. Although most of their tools were of stone, they also used wood and bone. A spearhead of yew, the oldest wooden implement in the world, was among the earlier finds at Clacton. The world for the people at Clacton was a leafy paradise, with dappled glades in woods of mixed oak which gave on to open country through which herds of wild horses galloped.

8   This wooden spearhead from Clacton-on-Sea, Essex, associated with flake tools of the 'Clactonian' industry, is the oldest wooden implement in the world. It dates from around 250,000 years ago

Planes and hand-axes

Tools of the type found at Clacton have been found else-where in southern Britain, notably at Henley in Oxfordshire and Swanscombe in Kent. They were probably still in fashion when a new type of tool stole the stage of implement evolution – the hand-axe. Of all Palaeolithic tools, hand-axes are the most characteristic. The later examples are often beautifully worked in oval, heart-shaped or pointed forms, which show a natural understanding of the quality of flint.

9 Clactonian chopper core from Highfields Gravel Pit, Henley-on-Thames, Oxford-shire. Such tools are among the earliest found in Britain

0   1   2   3   4   5 cm

Such tools are regarded by prehistorians as typical of what is known as the 'Acheulian industry', and have been found on a wide variety of sites in southern Britain. As far as is known from their distribution human settlement did not extend further west or north than a line roughly drawn from Scarborough to Plymouth. The richest hunting grounds for modern hand-axe enthusiasts have been the gravels of the

100ft terrace of the Thames (Boyn Hill Terrace). No fewer than 3,000 separate findspots of lower Palaeolithic implements have been recorded in Britain.

Past and present meet at Booker airport, near High Wycombe, Bucks. Planes take off and come in to land on an airstrip composed, in part, of lower Palaeolithic hand-axes. One of the finest examples found in the Thames valley gravels was picked up on a dump of gravel on the airfield which had been brought from the Henley gravel pit. When

10 Early Acheulian hand-axe (*bottom*) and unfinished rough-out for another Acheulian axe from Highfields Gravel Pit, Henley. Notice in the upper example the wear through being water-rolled

0   1   2   3   4   5 cm

the Highlands (Henley) gravel pit was at its operational peak in the 1950s, prehistorians could be seen sitting at one end of the conveyor belt picking off hand-axes as they went past. In an afternoon in 1962 one of the present authors found several hand-axes and an assortment of flake tools along with a Clactonian chopper core lying among the piles of gravel in the then silent pit. The sheer quantity of Palaeolithic hand-axes attests the industry of generation after generation of stone-age inhabitants in the Thames valley.

11 Lower Palaeolithic flake tools from Highfields, Henley-on-Thames. Notice the cortex (outer skin of the flint nodule) still apparent on part of each of these tools. They probably belong to the late middle Acheulian

Whence came the Clactonian and Acheulian toolmakers to Britain? Many experts believe that the manufacturers of 'Clacton' implements favoured fairly wooded areas and spread across from northern Europe. In contrast, the Acheulian workers preferred more open areas and had migrated northwards from Africa, perhaps through Spain. Acheulian types of axes are very widespread – they occur as far afield as Africa, India and the southern Caucasus, as well as much of Europe.

12 This superb late middle Acheulian hand-axe from Henley, Oxfordshire, was designed to have a spatulate or truncated end. Such axes are perhaps the most typical of all lower Palaeolithic tools (though they are more frequently of oval or pointed form). Date *c*.200,000 BC

```
0    1    2    3    4    5 cm
```

The first ancient Briton

One of the richest sites for producing hand-axes is at Swanscombe, Kent. It was here that the remains of the earliest human fossil in Britain came to light. Ardent feminists can be forgiven if they object to the lady concerned being called Swanscombe Man in archaeological literature. Only the skull has been discovered; two fragments of it were found in 1935–6, the remaining piece turning up in 1955 not many yards from the first findspot. Amazingly, the pieces fitted together like a jig-saw. The Swanscombe lady was probably in her early twenties when she died; her remains are now nearly a quarter of a million years old. Although at least 100,000 years younger than the fossil found at Vértesszöllös, Hungary, the Swanscombe example is still numbered among the earliest remains of *Homo sapiens* ever discovered.

Thanks to intensive research in the gravel pit in which the pieces came to light, a clear picture of the world of Swanscombe Man can be established. The fossil belongs to a fairly late stage in the lower Palaeolithic, when the hand-axe industries were well under way. The river Thames at this time had many channels, and wandered through a broad flood plain. Here was the perfect region for hunters; the diversity of environments – swamp, woodland, grassland and open water offered a rich variety of game. Ox and horse were in fairly abundant supply. Swanscombe Man probably lived in one of the camp sites that the hand-axe users tended to occupy on low-lying areas near their water supply. At night the woman whose fossil is now so famous would have

been able to huddle up close to the camp fire (Swanscombe has provided the earliest evidence for fire in Britain – some of the axes found near the skull showed signs of burning), knowing she was safe from the predators that prowled the edge of the camp – cave bear, wolf and lion. Unknown to her, the cool weather that caused her to draw her furs closer would have been due to the onset of a glacial period. The long millennia when hand-axes were the most important tools were coming to an end.

13 Two fragments of a skull of *Homo sapiens* found at Swanscombe, Kent. These are the earliest human fossils found in Britain, and were associated with Acheulian tools. They are among the earliest *Homo sapiens* fossils in Europe

No structures have been found at Swanscombe, but at Stoke Newington in Greater London in the nineteenth century Worthington Smith discovered a working floor where hand-axes had been made. Here he found a bed of ferns and the impressions where the poles of a windbreak had stood. At Caddington, Beds., a pile of discarded flakes was put together to form a 'mould' into which he poured plaster. Like one of the ghostly plaster bodies from Pompeii, a hand-axe emerged when he peeled off the flakes, conjured out of nothing, a shadow from the past.

14 This imaginative reconstruction recaptures life in the
time of Swanscombe Man.
However, in view of the cold
climate at the time, it seems
likely that the inhabitants of
Britain wore clothes, despite
the absence of evidence. These
would have been made of
skins

The lower to middle Palaeolithic

In the Scottish folk-song 'The Three Craws' it emerges that
of the trio of crows sitting on a wall, the third is not there at
all. Of the three phases of the Palaeolithic in Britain, the
middle one hardly appears to be there either.

Towards the end of the period when Acheulian axes were
in fashion, flint-workers devised a new method of making
tools. This technique is named after a French site – the
Levallois – and involved preparing the tool carefully on the
core before detaching it. The core of flint was thus left with a
distinctive 'tortoise' shape and the tool with a facetted butt.
It was costly on flint, but the results were flake implements
which could either be long and narrow or short and broad,
and which required no further retouch, as the edges were
razor sharp. Although pioneered in the warm (Hoxnian)
interglacial, the technique did not really catch on until the
onset of the next Ice Age, but once in fashion it remained in
use through that period and into the next warm interglacial.
The Levallois tool-makers may have been specialists in
mammoth hunting. At Ealing a Levallois flake was found
inside the remains of such a beast, while mammoth bones
were found with Levallois tools at Baker's Hole, Kent, and at
Brundon, Suffolk.

A similarly prepared core technique was used on the Continent by the hero of middle Palaeolithic archaeology in Europe, Neanderthal Man, who on occasion also used the Levallois technique. Prepared cores were, however, just one feature of Neanderthal flint-work which is grouped together under the label of 'Mousterian'.

No fossil remains of Neanderthal Man have been found in Britain, but the presence of distinctive Mousterian tools suggests strongly that some of these men at least wandered

15   These flakes, from High Lodge, Mildenhall, Suffolk, are typical of various flake industries which appeared towards the end of the lower Palaeolithic. High Lodge was a lakeside settlement occupied during an interstadial in the Wolstonian glaciation. The flake tools have been compared with those from La Micoque in France, and have been termed 'Proto-Charentian', but some have seen them as a development of Clactonian traditions, or even a specialized product of Acheulian axe-makers.

the woods and plains that could be found during the warmer periods of the last great Ice Age (70,000 to 8000 BC). In these periods the climate of Britain was probably akin to that of modern Finland, with birch, pine and spruce forests dominating the landscape. Mousterian implements have come to light in caves as far apart as Torbryan in south-east Devon and Pontnewydd in north Wales. The earliest Mousterian tools are distinctively heart-shaped axes, which French prehistorians have termed *bout coupé* (truncated butt). A series have been found at Little Paxton in Huntingdonshire, associated with arctic types of animals which suggest that Neanderthalers ventured into Britain in an early cold spell as well.

57

16 (a and b) These cordiform (i.e. heart-shaped) hand-axes are typical of the so-called Mousterian industry in France. The tools of this middle Palaeolithic industry were probably fashioned by *Homo neanderthalensis* – Neanderthal Man – though no actual fossil remains of Neanderthalers have come to light in Britain, and Mousterian tools are rare. These come from Coygan Cave, Laugharne, Dyfed

Most Mousterian tools can be assigned to one particular warm period when life sounds really rather idyllic. There was a copious supply of meat on the hoof – herds of bison, reindeer and mammoth roamed the open grassy plains and the scattered stretches of pine and birch woodland. The hunters may have followed the migrating animals from what is now the Continent. The assemblages of tools from this phase can be compared closely with finds from France. Heart-shaped axes were still fashionable, but now there were other typical tools in addition – side scrapers, points, blades with their backs blunted by secondary flaking and fine denticulated or toothed tools. They are not common, and their occurrence in caves such as Wookey Hole in Somerset, Pontnewydd in north Wales or Robin Hood's Cave in the Creswell Crags of Derbyshire seems to imply that caves and rock shelters were used seasonally by scattered bands of hunters.

The golden age of the caveman – the upper Palaeolithic in Britain
Compared with, for instance, those of France or Spain, the remains of upper Palaeolithic man in Britain are pathetically

few and unimpressive. It is none the less fascinating that from meagre pieces of material evidence surprising amounts of information can be gained or inferred about life in this remote time.

Most of the finds from the British upper Palaeolithic come from caves. This last sentence might evoke at once a picture (tenacious even in the archaeologist's mind from the museum displays of his youth) of a fur-clad lout roasting mammoth steaks at the mouth of a damp deep cave, while one of his fellows daubs pictures on the back wall in the hope that the next day's hunting might be good. It is probable, however, that caves were only one of many types of upper Palaeolithic home. The cold climate would have made them desirable residences, but not everyone would have been lucky enough to find one that was suitable; shallow rock-shelters that were formed from sea erosion, for instance, are far from ideal for prolonged occupation. But there are few remains of any 'open' settlements from the period in Britain. If they existed, the traces would have been slight in the first place, and easily destroyed by subsequent geological events. From the discoveries at sites such as Avdeevo and Molodova in Russia or Dolní Věstonice in Czechoslovakia it is known that upper Palaeolithic mammoth-hunters lived in tents and huts consisting of mammoth bone or tusk frameworks covered with skins. Although it is dangerous to make such inferences from negative evidence, perhaps it is reasonable to assume that such dwellings could well have been part of the landscape in Britain too.

That this inference is correct would seem to be confirmed by the finds made at Hengistbury Head in Dorset, where an upper Palaeolithic camp site was excavated in 1957 and again in 1968–9. There was some evidence that a tent had been erected here, its edges weighted by stones (large cores left after tool-making). It was approximately oval, about 6m by 5m in extent, and had what may have been hearths within it.

The evidence suggests that the caves favoured by British Palaeolithic Man were those with relatively narrow entrances, with occupation being concentrated in the front. The clues from France and Spain suggest that cave paintings, the great achievement of upper Palaeolithic Man, were executed in inner recesses – they were, in the widest sense, 'shrines'. Cave paintings are totally absent in Britain. There are a number of explanations for this. The caves in which paintings have been found are subterranean and have been sealed from the outer air until their discovery in recent

Map 1
Pleistocene Britain

land mass at time of Devensian advance

edge of ice sheet at its greatest extent (Wolstonian glacial)

edge of ice in Devensian advance

times. The first cave paintings were found as late as 1879 at Altamira in Spain (though some were probably revealed but not recognized some years before), and most of the discoveries of Palaeolithic mural art have come to light this century. The tragic decay of the paintings found at Lascaux, France, in 1940 emphasizes how rapidly such works can perish when exposed to air. If paintings existed in the British caves known to have been occupied by Palaeolithic Man, they would almost certainly have vanished centuries ago. The more optimistic amongst us, however, may take heart that it is not impossible that one day a pot-holer will discover a sealed cave in Britain with frescoes as fine as those from Altamira, Lascaux, Les Trois Frères or Le Tuc d'Audoubert in Spain and France. One other factor must be borne in mind. In the Palaeolithic period, Britain was the outer limit of the occupied world. The population of what is now southern England could never have been large, and the finds from British caves indicate that their long-dead owners were very much the poor cousins of the inhabitants of the Dordogne in the same period.

The finds from the upper Palaeolithic in Britain belong to two periods in the last great Ice Age, a slightly warmer one and the last cold one of which the chief culture is named the Creswellian, after the type-site in Derbyshire.

During the earlier of the two periods the landscape through which the fur-clad pioneers roamed was fairly open. The sparse horizon was relieved by scattered juniper, willow, pine and birch. Against the skyline food, in the shape of horse, reindeer, red deer, giant Irish deer, bison, woolly rhinoceros and mammoth, or danger, in the guise of lion, wolf, bear or hyena, would have been easily visible. For the first time in Palaeolithic archaeology, radio-carbon dates are a help, and point to the first settlers trudging across the land-bridge that became the English Channel around 27,000–26,000 BC.

The caves that have provided hints of habitation at this time are scattered quite widely – Fynnon Bueno in Clwyd, Paviland in the Gower peninsular, Kent's Cavern near Torquay and the Creswell Crags of Derbyshire have all yielded tools of this period. Typical of these were leaf-shaped missile heads, and a type of tool known as a 'busked burin' which was common in France.

Perhaps to this time belongs the most famous Palaeolithic burial in Britain – the Red Lady of Paviland, which was found by Dean Buckland and wrongly identified as Romano-British (p. 15). As if to balance the mistaken identity of Swanscombe Man, this is now known to have been a young man who had been covered in red ochre. Was this a symbol of blood, or a pathetic gesture of hope for a life after death? The Paviland youth was laid to rest wearing a necklace of animal teeth extracted from the jaws of wolf and reindeer. The Goat's Hole (the local name for the cave), in contrast to others mentioned in this book, is coastal and opens out from a thirty-foot high cleft in the precipitous cliffs. When a film crew were attempting to obtain the right light for filming the wartime propaganda film *The Beginnings of History* the entire team was trapped by the tide and forced to swim to safety. In its time of occupation, however, the cave was far from the coast.

There are many incredible stories of one part of an object being found and years later another section turning up on almost the same spot. How could it have been missed the first time? The Swanscombe skull was one such example, and another came to light in the Goat's Hole. Here Dean Buckland found a deformed tusk of a mammoth with a piece cut from it. A century later the missing piece appeared. It had been carved in antiquity into an egg-shaped pendant. But it was not merely any piece of the tusk that had been chosen. Surely this must be one of the most obscure materials ever chosen for a piece of jewellery – 'an osseous growth produced in a wound in the pulp cavity'.

The dancing man of the Creswell Crags

By about 25,000 years ago, had thermometers been invented they would have been recording a marked fall in temperature once more. Britain was gripped by an ice sheet and the few brave humans who had inhabited the area now abandoned it to nature, seeking warmer haunts further south. About 14,000 years ago conditions improved and by around 10,000 BC Britain was once more 'home' to Palaeolithic hunters.

Although southern Britain was habitable, it was not the kind of place that travel brochures might describe lyrically. Park tundra prevailed, with some woodland in sheltered places. Horse, reindeer and elk made up the main food supply; mammoth, woolly rhinoceros, hyena and lion were extinct species.

The late Palaeolithic hunters were still predominantly cave dwellers. They had wandered from the north European plain and though used to pursuing the herds of game across open land, once established in Britain they seem to have changed their habits and started to explore the upland environment, albeit on a seasonal basis. Whereas in northern Europe and France reindeer herds were the staple food supply, in Britain horses were a more readily available source of protein. It is probable, but not provable, that this period saw the beginnings of animal herding and possibly even domestication. A carving of the time from St Michel d'Arudy in France seems to show a horse with a bridle, and in parts of eastern England the rich charcoal content of the soil laid down at this time suggests extensive forest fire, perhaps started by men to drive the herds or to open up fresh grazing grounds. The British caves may have been occupied

17 The entrance to Paviland Cave, Pembroke. Now on the coast, in upper Palaeolithic times it was further inland, and is typical of the occupied caves of upper Palaeolithic Britain. Among the finds from this site was the famous 'Red Lady of Paviland', a (male) ochre burial discovered by Dean Buckland in the nineteenth century

seasonally in the pursuit of reindeer herds. Evidence from Tornewton Cave, Devon suggests that it was occupied in spring and early summer only.

This last phase of the British Palaeolithic is well represented in the finds from the caves of the Creswell Crags of Derbyshire and as a result is termed by prehistorians the *Creswellian*. The characteristic toolkit of a well-equipped handyman of the time comprised large numbers of 'angle-backed blades', steeply retouched awls, burins and end-scrapers. Although the British tools are distinctive, similar types are found on the Continent in Germany and the Low Countries, where they are datable to the period *c*. 12,000–8800 BC. This ties in neatly with the dates from British sites where Creswellian tools have been found which go down to 8000 BC or slightly later.

In the Creswellian phase for the first time prehistorians have a varied collection of bone-work as well as flints to study. Harpoons fashioned of reindeer antler, with one or two rows of savage barbs, are very similar to those from the classic French cave sites, and have been found in Britain in such places as Aveline's Hole in the Mendips and Kent's Cavern. From Gough's Cave in Cheddar, Somerset, has come an ivory rod that may have been part of a bow, for it would seem that the bow and arrow made its début in history around this time.

Cheddar Gorge is central to all discussions of upper Palaeolithic Man in Britain. This is a strange place in the British landscape – one moment the visitor is in bright sunshine in the village of Cheddar, and then within seconds is dwarfed by the rising cliffs of limestone which overshadow cars that seem like mere toys. Here and there as the road winds its way through the Gorge, cave mouths open, with their entrances obscured by modern buildings with turnstiles. No matter how many cars or holiday-makers, Cheddar Gorge manages to stay suffocatingly grand and it is a relief to pass out of it into the world of modern man.

Of the Cheddar caves, Gough's is the most spectacular, and has on display a collection of finds from within. They include the bones of what is called Cheddar Man (he is just another *Homo sapiens* like ourselves) whose burial was one of several of the late Palaeolithic that have been found in Britain. Two extraordinary and puzzling *batons de commandement* were discovered here – handled antler objects with a single perforation at the broad end. What were they? Staffs of office? Ritual clubs? Spear-shaft straighteners? One can but guess. Sewing needles dropped in the cave by an ancient tailor or sempstress remind us that clothes were a necessity in those cold times – modern cartoons are usually quite inaccurate on this subject. Yet another bone presents a puzzle. It appears to be a borer, but along its length are carefully cut notches. Perhaps it is a tally, used to keep a check on how many horses had been killed, or how many skins remained for making into the latest fashion. Or is it, as has been suggested, connected with some lunar calendrical calculations, thought necessary for predicting the migration times of beasts and birds?

It is to Creswell, however, that one must turn for evidence of upper Palaeolithic art. A few meagre pieces of bone are Britain's only contribution to this, one of the greatest periods of artistic flowering the world has ever known. The artist who produced the Creswell doodles was not even a Palaeolithic Hogarth to France and Spain's Monet or

Picasso. But one feature of British art is here – line drawing rather than painting. Even in this remote age when artists must have had to starve in caves rather than garrets, it was line not colour that was favoured. The better of the two Creswell bone engravings is a lightly incised sketch of a horse's head and shoulders. It is not up to Stubbs, but it is not bad, and certainly captured something of the nature of the beast. Mark it well, for better will not be seen in the time-span covered by this book. It came from Robin Hood's

Cave. The second engraving, from Pin Hole Cave, is less inspired. It has been interpreted as a 'masked male dancer' but it looks more like a knock-kneed goat having difficulty with trousers that are far too tight. Such engravings invite comparison with, for instance, the 'dancing sorcerer of Les Trois Frères'. But alas recent research has shown that this celebrated figure was as much a figment of its recorder's fertile imagination as an actuality – only the eye of faith can discern it amongst the maze of superimposed pictures of which it forms a part. However, there is some other evidence for the use of animal masks in upper Palaeolithic ritual, so perhaps the orthodox interpretation of the illustration may be reasonably correct. If so, it leaves the twentieth-century mind plenty of scope for musing on the nature of Palaeolithic art and rites about which it is arguable that more nonsense has been written than on anything except perhaps megaliths.

So much for the remains of upper Palaeolithic Man in Britain – a handful of bone tools, an assortment of chipped flints, a couple of sketches scratched on bone and the remains of a few mortals. The line-up is unimpressively sparse; but in those far-off times Britain was not encumbered by over-population. The entire upper Palaeolithic

18 There are only a few authenticated upper Palaeolithic carvings in Britain, in contrast to the wealth of upper Palaeolithic art in France. This rib-bone is engraved with a very naturalistic horse head, and comes from Robin Hood's Cave, Creswell, Derbyshire. Actual size

19 What has been interpreted as a 'dancing sorcerer' appears lightly engraved on this bone from Pin Hole Cave, Creswell, Derbyshire. It has its counterparts in France (such as the 'sorcerer of Les Trois Frères'). It perhaps dates from around 12,000 BC

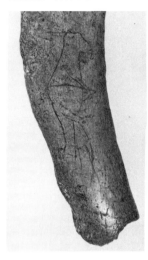

community at any one time might have been in the region of 250 souls.

Yet these few upper Palaeolithic men made important contributions to the development of human society. Never before or since has such economic specialization to meet the environment been carried out so effectively. It could be argued that had it not been for the Palaeolithic hunters pursuing the migrating herds of reindeer and horse, animal domestication might not have come about. Not until the Renaissance did art again approach the realism and feeling for nature displayed by the Continental cave artists. With the gradual retreat of the ice sheets, the old order crumbled. Art apparently passed away to be replaced by a jumble of squiggles and dots which was the best to which Mesolithic man could aspire. The migrating herds moved northwards behind the shrinking ice and in their wake forests grew up. It was in these woodlands that the Mesolithic hunters sought their game and from the seas and rivers swollen by the melt-waters that they drew their harvests of fish and shells.

The Mesolithic – Britain in transition

The climate began to improve around 12,000 BC and, with a slight set-back in the ninth millennium BC, continued to get warmer until around 3200 BC when Britain was appreciably more fortunate in its weather than it is now.

Even before the ice had receded, however, man had had some impact on the British environment – for instance, he had successfully exterminated the lion, elephant and hippo, though of course we cannot tell whether this was a deliberate policy or not.

The birch and pine that covered Britain at the beginning of the post-glacial era gave way around 7500 BC to mixed oak forest with hazel and pine trees. Some time after this the continuing rise in sea level severed Britain from the Continent with the formation of the English Channel. Mixed oak forest still dominated the landscape and alder was becoming more common. Meanwhile what had long been an extension of the north European plain was sinking under what is now sailed as the North Sea. These changes in sea level came about through the ice melting, releasing long-imprisoned waters.

The growth of forest meant a change in hunting habits for man. The game to be found in the dense woodland was of a lighter build than the lumbering herds of the upper Palaeolithic. Red deer and aurochs (the extinct wild ox) provided the main food supply. The forests abounded with creatures who live in Britain today – polecat, squirrel and pine marten for instance. The rivers teemed with tasty fish and water fowl. After the lean millennia, this was abundance indeed.

The masters of this forest environment were the Maglemosians, named after one of their many settlements in Denmark which is called Magle Mose (literally 'the big bog'). They packed their leather bags and crossed the land before it became submerged beneath the North Sea. On one such migration some careless individual dropped a barbed point which was by chance recovered from a lump of moorlog by the shipping vessel *Colinda*, 25 miles off the Norfolk coast.

20 Mesolithic flint-work of Maglemosian type. The large flint at the top is an 'axe rejuvenator' struck off an axe when the cutting edge was too battered to chop effectively. It and the flake (*bottom left*) come from Victoria Park, Newbury, Berkshire. The small flint at the bottom right is a 'micro-burin', which, despite its name, is not a tool but the waste product left after preparing a flake by a specialist method. Its patina is cracked and heat-crazed – it was found in a hearth at Thatcham, Berkshire

```
0     1     2     3     4     5 cm
```

The Maglemosians must have spent much of their lives in a green forest twilight. They fashioned a few stone axes to help them cut their way through lighter woodlands. The rest of their toolkit comprised very small flints indeed – the microliths so characteristic of Mesolithic communities. These were mounted up in wooden hafts to make composite tools such as saws or knives. Engraving tools for the working of antler and bone have been found. The 'micro-burins' that are sometimes encountered are in fact the waste product from making microliths by a very specialized technique which involved notching a blade and then snapping it off. The bone harpoon points of the Maglemosians are distinctive. When a Maglemosian wished to grub up plants he reached for a perforated mattock of elk antler, despite the increasing rarity of this animal.

Star Carr in Yorkshire provides such a vivid insight into Maglemosian life that it is as if for the first time a TV camera has filmed the past. It was the rather prosaic discovery of some flint implements and a few pieces of decayed antler and bone that provided the clue to the existence of the site when a field drain was being cut in 1949. The excavation started in that year was so meticulous and the remains so well preserved that it was possible to reconstruct life and the environment round the settlement unusually fully. At the lakeside campsite about twenty-five people (five of whom were men capable of hunting) had lived on a seasonal basis. The workers had constructed a platform of logs on the edge of the lake. From the way in which the trunks were lying it was somewhat eerily possible to determine the way in which they had been felled by the axeman. The camp had been in occupation during winter and spring, when the hunters had enjoyed menus that included such delicacies as red deer, roe deer, elk, ox and pig in that order of popularity. The bones of pine marten, hedgehog, hare, badger, fox and beaver showed the wide variety of wild-life around the settlement.

Radio-carbon dating showed that the humans were active at Star Carr around 7600 bc, a date which more or less coincides with those of the other Maglemosian sites in Britain. The remarkable conditions led to the preservation of organic remains that rarely survive elsewhere, in particular wooden objects. A wooden paddle, for instance, would undoubtedly have been used to manoeuvre a canoe made from a hollowed-out oak log. Men paddling their way along waterways in similar craft must have been commonplace sights in early prehistoric Britain. A series of tightly bound rolls of birch bark should have been used on the site as fuel, or more probably as a source of resin for mounting microliths, but for some reason they were not, and have survived to the present day. The craftsmen worked antler by the 'groove and splinter' method, whereby two slanting grooves were engraved with a sharp flint and the resulting segment splintered off. Bone awls and pins were common possessions of the people of Star Carr. Most intriguing of all were the antler 'frontlets' which it can only be assumed were the accepted dress at ritual dances. The form closely recalls the head-dresses worn in English folk customs, notably the Abbots Bromley Horn Dance. This festival, unique in Europe, is celebrated on the Monday after the first Sunday after 4 September in the Staffordshire village. Six deer-men (three black, three white) perform a highly formalized dance or 'running' in which they confront one another, holding wooden replicas of deer heads with horns attached. A bowman then pretends to stalk them, shooting imaginary arrows. The deer horns on the wooden heads are themselves very ancient, and were reputedly brought from Scandinavia over a thousand years ago. They are of reindeer, not red deer, and thus particularly appropriate to a ritual dance which may originate in Mesolithic or even upper Palaeolithic times. The Star Carr frontlets remind the observer of the engravings of the 'dancing man' of the Creswell Crags.

In the eighth millennium BC any Maglemosians or similar forest dwellers would have had to travel considerable distances before they reached another settlement that was 'just like home'. It is highly likely that the community at Star Carr would have ranged through 200 square miles of woodlands without meeting other humans. By extension, these calculations imply that the population in Britain at the time numbered very roughly 10,000 people. The 200 square miles of forest would have supported approximately 3,400 red deer, even though, compared to the upper Palaeolithic period, meat was in fairly sparse supply. Allowing fifty animals per annum as a reasonable protein intake per person, the community could have been supplied with enough venison alone to prevent fear of starvation.

Tools used by the Maglemosians have been found as far afield as Cornwall, Somerset and the southern Pennines, as well as Yorkshire and various sites in the south and east such as Thatcham, Berkshire. A few years ago it was possible to enjoy the flowers in Victoria Park, Newbury, Berkshire, while surreptitiously observing vestiges of Maglemosian hunters. The flower beds near the bandstand yielded to an eagle eye their tools, or even the bones of *bos primigenius* (the aurochs or wild oxen) that they hunted. In Wales and Scotland similar tool assemblages indicate that groups of people lived a similar way of life somewhat later in time. Around 6000 BC or slightly later the first Mesolithic settlers were moving their families and belongings into Scotland. They set up home at least in Morton in Fife and Lussa Bay on Jura. Never before in prehistory had men ventured so far north.

The Maglemosians were not the only inhabitants of Mesolithic Britain, but their colleagues or rivals can mainly be detected through objects. Sometime before the end of the seventh millennium BC, for instance, new types of microliths were being used. These are of neat, geometric shapes such as trapezes, scalene triangles and crescents, and are on narrow blades as opposed to the broader Maglemosian examples. Considerable variation can be detected in the assemblages from different places, but broadly speaking it is possible to distinguish between sites which produce ex-

21 Extremes of Mesolithic flint-working can be seen in these examples from Sussex. The tool on the left is a microlith, which was probably mounted up with others into a composite tool. The large flint is an axe of a type found in south-east England and known as a 'Thames pick' – it was probably used for forest clearance

clusively geometric microliths, and those which yield a mixture of geometric microliths and larger, non-geometric flint tools. The latter are found mainly in southern and eastern Britain, the former predominantly in the north. The new types of flints seem to have been a development in response to new needs in missiles, and it is not at all clear whether they were introduced by newcomers from Belgium and Holland, or were a local invention. These geometric microliths continued to be made for thousands of years. It seems very probable that similar Mesolithic bands were using them for hunting in the shrinking forests, after the farmer of the following archaeological period had arrived in Britain – radio-carbon dates for sites producing geometric microliths go down to 3000 BC or even later. On a couple of sites, for example Shewalton Moor, Ayrshire, and Risby Warren, Lincolnshire, the 'Mesolithic' hunters even attempted to copy Neolithic arrowheads.

Some Mesolithic people were not forest dwellers, but specialist fishermen, who eked out their living on the coast of western Scotland. Sometimes referred to as 'Obanian' after the discoveries made in caves at Oban in the nineteenth century, they have left more evidence of their lives on the islands of Oronsay in the Inner Hebrides, and Risga on Loch Sunart. Radio-carbon dates assign them to the fifth–fourth millennium BC. Their insalubrious-sounding trade-mark was a coastal midden – a huge mound of discarded shells, tools and other rubbish. Their most characteristic artefact was a specialist implement which has been termed a 'limpet scoop', and was perhaps used for scraping the unappetising shellfish off rocks. Their other stone tools were crude, and comprised mainly rough scrapers. The Obanians, however, were relatively accomplished at working bone and antler. Their tool-bags would have included barbed harpoon-heads and mattock-heads, the latter made from red-deer antler.

It was the Mesolithic hunters who began the long process of drastically changing the landscape of Britain. Today the North Yorkshire Moors are largely treeless and barren. In Mesolithic times they were wooded, until man gradually attacked them. Oddly enough, it was not the axe-wielding Maglemosians who were primarily responsible, but the axe-less makers of geometric tools, who had no doubt carried out their own primitive time-and-motion studies and ruthlessly cleared the land with fire. Charcoal is one form of evidence for the human use of fire at this stage. Another is the slight increase in birch and hazel, which tend to spread into fire-cleared areas and are themselves fairly resistant to flames.

Why should such huntsmen wish to open up the forest which sheltered the game upon which they depended? There is no certain answer, but one seems likely: within the forest there would have been open glades, where animals (and man) came for water. It followed logically that if a wider area were opened up, more animals could come to drink and therefore more food would be readily available. The opening up of woodland would also have facilitated the rounding up and perhaps corralling of game. The herding of animals, notably deer, is very likely to have taken place in Mesolithic Britain.

But the effect of fire would have upset the natural pattern of the vegetation cover. In some cases the destruction of the trees which naturally soak up moisture would have led to water-logging. Impoverishment of the soil would have followed, too, as trees are essential for the cycling of nutrients. Had herds of animals been compounded, the ground would have been compacted. Fire would itself have impoverished the soil, and thus would have set in motion a natural cycle which at its most extreme would have ended up in the formation of blanket bog.

In the south a similar story can be told. At Iping, Sussex, the destruction of a hazel woodland by Maglemosian farmers led to soil deterioration, wind erosion and the formation of heathland.

With forest clearance and deliberate herding the Mesolithic people were coming close to one of the major landmarks in human history – the development of farming. This phenomenon is usually associated with the Neolithic period when it became fully effective. It is not surprising to find out that the Maglemosians had domesticated at least one animal – the dog. A natural scavenger around human settlements, it would have been the ideal companion on hunting expeditions, and may even have been used in the herding of game. The earliest domesticated dog known in the world was found at Star Carr. It was a true dog, but was clearly descended from a domesticated wolf. Because of the long survival of many Mesolithic cultures, it is not certain whether some late communities learned about domestication from incoming farmers, or whether they may have begun domestication of their own accord. There is no reason why the latter should not have come about. In the absence of botanical evidence, it is not possible to determine whether any attempt to 'harvest' wild plants was made in Mesolithic Britain, but it is not inherently impossible. The Mesolithic Natufians of Palestine certainly systematically harvested wild crops as an important part of their diet, even though they do not appear to have cultivated them. It is noteworthy that they used sickles with blades composed of microliths set in a haft – could the British microliths have also been used for harvesting some kind of plant (albeit not cereal, since wild cereals did not grow in Britain)?

To assess how far Palaeolithic or Mesolithic food-gatherers might in favourable conditions develop their culture, one need only study a site such as Lepenski Vir in Yugoslavia. This Mesolithic settlement was occupied by fishermen who were able to stay in one place without roaming the forest in search of food. They built a village of trapezoidal houses for a hundred or more people, and carved stone sculptures, notably of human heads with fish-like features. Although the Danube provided most of their food, they also gathered plants from the surrounding forest.

However, these changes in economics that occurred towards the end of the Mesolithic period were no cultural revolution. The gradual transition from herding and crop-gathering to farming was not an enormous one for the Mesolithic inhabitants of Britain, though it was lasting. It was a natural step forwards and was not necessarily enforced by waves of Neolithic immigrants as was once thought. The time-scale is long and the abandonment of an itinerant way of life was gradual and apparently due as much to a natural development within the islands as to incomers: the Mesolithic period faded out slowly.

Chapter three

The revolutionaries – Man tames the environment (Neolithic)

'Shirtless' was a forger. How he acquired this alias is not known, though he also went by the names of 'Fossil Willy', 'Cockney Bill', 'Bones' and 'the Antiquarian'. It is however as 'Flint Jack' that he gained notoriety in prehistoric studies, for his greatest masterpieces were forged flint tools. He was born Edward Simpson, near Whitby in 1815. Acquaintance with well-known local collectors soon furnished him with a trade – fossil-hunting in the Scarborough, Filey and Bridlington area, to supply them with specimens. He soon discovered that flint implements fetched a good price, and when real ones eluded him, he took to making his own. He travelled round the country selling his wares, moving on when things became too 'hot' for him. Scotland and Ireland he avoided, as the people were 'too cannie'.

By 1860 Flint Jack's expertise was known far and wide. In that year he was invited to demonstrate his prowess at flint-working to the Geologist's Association in London. He accepted, and on the platform

> He undid the knots of his red handkerchief, which proved to be full of fragments of flint. He turned them over and selected a small piece which he held, sometimes on his knee, sometimes in the palm of his hand, and gave it a few careless blows with what looked like a crooked nail. In a few minutes he had produced a small arrowhead, which he handed to a gentleman near . . . his fragments of flint were fast converted into different varieties of arrowheads, and exchanged for sixpences among the audience (J. Stevens, 1894).

Flint Jack was jealous of his skill. On hearing that Sir John Evans was adept at producing flint implements, the forger visited him to find out whether 'he was likely to attain an equal degree of eminence with himself'. Eventually Flint Jack took to drink – by this time his tools were so famous that few people were taken in by him and he died in prison, a pauper.

By the 1850s flint forging was a popular and profitable pastime. Snake Willy, alias Skin and Grief (a Yorkshireman despite the fact that his alias sounds like Cockney rhyming slang) was a master of the decade, while at Stoke Newington in the 1890s flint forgery was a local industry. The Stoke Newington craftsmen knew, like modern forgers of antique furniture, that patina was important. They shook up their copies in sacks with other stones and sand, and boiled them in saucepans with old rusty nails, fragments of iron, etc.

Worthington Smith, who made a study of the Stoke Newington forgers, pointed out a moral in his tale. 'It is a curious fact . . .', he wrote in 1894, 'that some of the collectors who informed the workmen of the points of authenticity in stone tools were themselves severely bitten by the forgers. This fact should delight the hearts of all antiquaries.'

It would seem that collectors, anxious that the 'finders' of the tools would notice the most desirable specimens, 'lent the men their best genuine tools as aids to discovery. . . . At first the forgeries were all dull and lustreless. On this fact being made known to the forgers, they vigorously brushed their forgeries all over with a very hard brush; the result was an excellent and natural looking lustre or polish.'

It can be concluded from the above that flint implements were easy to produce, a passable arrowhead being the work of less than a minute. Thus the vast array of flint implements that have survived from prehistoric Britain does not necess-arily imply a large population. One man could have produced thousands in a week – had he so desired – and still have had time to run his farm. It is also a salutary fact that Neolithic Britain is obviously what we want to make of it. The archaeological evidence contains a shoal of red herrings, and it is all too easy to be taken in by supposedly 'convincing' evidence for a theory if we wish to be bamboozled.

The sources

The surviving material evidence for Neolithic Britain is perhaps as varied as for any period in the prehistoric past. Not only are there stone tools in greater abundance and variety than ever before, but there is also pottery for the first time. Although there are of course no metal tools, quite a variety of bone implements exist, particularly from northern Scotland, and there are even a few wooden fragmentary bowls and implements.

Sites are varied, but many of them appear to be 'ritual' in the widest sense of the word. Some of these places are primarily funerary, though the distinctions between them and non-funerary sites are often minimal, as burials are found on both, and there is evidence for ritual as well as burial on funerary sites. Funerary monuments comprise various types of tomb used for the collective disposal of the dead – earthen long barrows and stone-built chambered tombs. Non-funerary monuments include 'causewayed camps', which, as well as having other possible functions, served as meeting places; henges, which were ritual circles; cursuses, which were linear earthworks; and, towards the end of the period, standing stones.

Houses and other domestic sites are relatively not well attested, except in the Northern Isles of Scotland. Comparatively little is known of the homes of the Neolithic farmers or their field systems, and the details of their economy have not yet been fully researched.

The Neolithic in Britain begins with the arrival of scattered groups of immigrants whose origins are still largely obscure, but lie in western Europe. They introduced plant cultivation and animal husbandry before 4000 BC and began to open up the forest for their fields. Almost nothing is known about the earliest phase for it was not until after 4000 BC that the farmers began to erect their characteristic monuments.

The early Neolithic people of Britain were active traders, marketing both pottery and stone axes over wide areas. Axes were produced in what have been termed axe factories, and where surface supplies of suitable stone were not available, mines were sunk to follow bands of fine flint. To facilitate such a trade, roads were built and waterways were undoubtedly important. Markets may have been held in the 'causewayed camps'. Stone axes are common finds around Neolithic ritual sites, suggesting that they were as vital to religious belief as they were to economics.

The early Neolithic people seem to have lived in small rectangular timber huts. Those at Carn Brea, Cornwall, and probably elsewhere, were sometimes protected behind a rampart.

In the early Neolithic the bodies of the dead were collected together and sometimes left to rot in 'mortuary houses' within enclosures, before being buried under a long earthen mound (a long barrow). Stone tombs built with megalithic (huge undressed) boulders overlap chronologically with the earthen long barrows, and some of the earliest may have been stone versions of the entrances to the timber-built enclosures, or perhaps of mortuary houses. Later influence probably from the Continent introduced more sophisticated types of megalithic tomb known as passage graves, in which a stone-built tunnel led to a chamber or chambers within the mound. Great diversity is observable among the chambered tombs of Britain, which fall into regional groups some of which influenced each other.

Radical changes came about in late Neolithic Britain after about 3000 BC. There is evidence that chiefdoms grew up, with powerful leaders who were able to organize the people to erect complex ritual structures such as the enormous 'henge' monuments. Examples of these are Durrington Walls in Wiltshire, or the mound of Silbury Hill in the same county which required 18 million man-hours to build. The growth of chiefdoms was contemporaneous with the acceleration of knowledge about astronomy and mathematics, and it has been suggested that Britain was ruled by priest-kings who kept the learning alive. In this period there is also evidence for economic changes, early Neolithic fields being abandoned to nature. Pigs, which are forest animals, were more important in the diet, as were wild fowl. This swing away from agriculture may have been due to the exhaustion of the soil in the lands farmed.

Contemporary with these late Neolithic developments was the arrival in Britain of the Beaker people who introduced new burial rites, pottery and metal-working. These are considered in the following chapter.

The origins of farming

Although the Mesolithic people may have made some headway towards inventing farming, the activity is still an important characteristic of the Neolithic period. It was not until this phase that the full impact of the new way of life was felt. But where did the idea originate?

The beginnings of farming can be traced to the Near East, where by accident of history and geography the wild ancestors of both domesticated animals and cultivated cereals were to be found in the same landscape. Despite extensive research, the actual origins of farming still remain very uncertain, due to the insubstantial nature of the evidence and the long stretches of time involved.* However it is clear that in Palestine from around 10,000 bc onwards, wild crops were being harvested, while not long after 7000 bc at Beidha in Jordan, goats were being domesticated and the plant remains of barley show the transition from wild to cultivated forms. Two thousand years earlier, at Zawi Chemi Shanidar, in Iraq, there are signs that sheep were being herded and possibly domesticated.

*Due to difficulties involved in re-calibrating dates before *c.* 5000 BC the dates given in this section are not calibrated – calendrical dates might be appreciably earlier. Uncalibrated dates are indicated by the convention bc.

The subsequent spread of farming was a prolonged process which lasted several thousand years. By the later seventh millennium farming communities were well established in Anatolia. Farmers built the mud-brick city of Çatal Hüyük, with its close-packed houses, its painted shrines to some unknown ox-deity, and (towards the end of its occupation) its fine burnished pottery. At Çatal Hüyük there are signs that copper was already being worked into beads, tubes and possibly even tools, at the time when Europe was still emerging from the Mesolithic – copper was not to be worked in Europe until nearly two thousand years later.

From Anatolia, farming spread to Greece, the Balkans and Crete before 6000 bc. By the fifth millennium it had moved northwards along the Danube into wetter, more densely forested lands, where timber rather than mud-brick was the favoured building material. The characteristic village comprised long, often trapezoidal houses with sloping roofs which were intended for more than a single family – some may have housed as many as a hundred people. The builders of these settlements are distinguished by their Linear pottery (incised with linear ornament) and their spread can be chronicled during the fifth millennium bc across the loess lands of central Europe to Germany and the Low Countries in one direction, and the Vistula and Dniestr in another. They tended to hack out the forest with their stone axes and then burn the stumps to enrich the fields thus formed. As the land became exhausted they moved on to found a new village, returning to the old on a cycle spread out over many years.

Meanwhile, farming had spread across the Mediterranean to Spain and western France. From coastal areas it spread inland into the rest of France, Switzerland and the north Italian lakes. It was well established in Iberia in the second half of the fifth millennium BC.

The stage was set for the arrival of farming proper in Britain. Sadly for prehistorians, almost nothing is known about the material possessions or lifestyles of the first farming colonists from the Continent – by the time the first pottery sherds can be distinguished they already show distinctively British characteristics and there are no other 'early' finds to pin-point the Continental homelands of the immigrants. Desperate scholars are thus forced to take up clues from slight similarities between pots found on each side of the Channel. The earliest ceramics found in Britain, for instance, belong to a large family of leathery, bag-shaped and virtually undecorated wares that go by the name of 'western Neolithic' in archaeological text-books. The British pots show certain features in common with some ceramics found in France. There are also hints of connections with a group of Neolithic peoples known as the Michelsberg culture. This is found in Belgium, northern France, the Rhineland and parts of Switzerland, and is partly related to the 'western Neolithic' cultures and partly to those of the Linear pottery people of central Europe and the 'Funnel-necked Beaker' people of the north European plain and Scandinavia.

First farmers in Britain

The earliest evidence for Neolithic settlers west of the English Channel comes not from England but from Ireland, where at Ballynagilly in Co. Tyrone a rectangular house built with stout uprights of timber and split-oak plank walling has been excavated. The settlement produced a radio-carbon date series going back to 4580 BC and the house appears to have been constructed around 4200–4000 BC.

Although as yet no Neolithic site in Britain has produced such early radio-carbon dates, it is highly likely that farming communities were established contemporaneously on both sides of the Irish Sea. At the time when the first substantial tombs and earthworks were being built in Britain, farming was sufficiently established to have an impact on the environment. Indeed, it is through the environmental changes brought about by the introduction of farming that the beginning of Neolithic Britain can be chronicled.

Before considering these, however, it is salutary to reflect that the advent of farming did not necessarily bring about a marked improvement in the standard of life. The hunting and gathering communities were almost certainly skilled specialists who had adapted their lifestyle to a particular economy and had it worked out to a fine art. If one type of food was in short supply they would have substituted another. The hunters at Star Carr, for instance, would hardly have had undue anxieties about food shortages. The problems of winter famines are as acute for food-gatherers as they are for food producers, though in a farming community crop failure or murrain amongst the cattle spells disaster for the people are not adapted to seeking what nature has to offer.

Thus did the beginnings of farming bring with it new evils. The settled life led to the growth of villages and larger communities, and where people are grouped together disease can spread rapidly. In a hunting and gathering society 'survival of the fittest' is a universal law. Now and again, as in the case of a Neanderthal burial at Shanidar in

22 This beautifully fashioned flint sickle proclaims the arrival of farming in Neolithic Britain. It was found in the Thames at Chelsea

Iraq, there are hints that the weak were succoured by the rest of the community, but it was a rare event in the past. With a more assured food supply due to farming, the infirm are more likely to survive, natural selection is upset and genetic defects can be passed on more readily. A further evil was toothache. The addition of cereal to the diet of farmers resulted in a marked increase in dental caries, for which Neolithic man can have had no effective answer.

Farming also brought new responsibilities. In the carefree days of the hunter and gatherer people travelled light, for they were constantly on the move to fresh hunting and cropping grounds. Personal property was a hindrance, and travel gear would have been confined to a tent or a canoe and essential tools or weapons. Once men had achieved the distinction of a fixed address, they had to accumulate property. There were livestock to guard, field systems to tend, houses to build and repair. Even if it is assumed that property was held in common by the community (which is far from certain) there would have been outsiders from neighbouring villages eager to avail themselves of stock or possessions. Raiding by marauding animals was not the only threat. Warfare and feuding would be natural results of envy and it is not surprising to find that the 'earliest murder victim' found in Britain was a Neolithic inhabitant of what is now Peterborough, or the earliest 'battlefield' was a Neolithic line of defence at Crickley Hill, Gloucestershire. Nevertheless, farming brought obvious advantages which had immediate impact upon the economy as well as on the health and happiness of farmers.

Economy and environment

In recent years, prehistorians have been much concerned with the *landnam*, a phase in which the forest of Mesolithic times was opened up to make way for field and pasture. It was noted that at this time there was a marked decline of elm pollens, which was believed to have been caused by the felling of elms to provide fodder for animals – elm leaves were known to have been used on the Continent for this purpose during the Neolithic period. The recent outbreak of Dutch Elm Disease in Britain, however, may call this theory into question – could there have been a similar disaster around 3000 BC? This seems increasingly likely. It is difficult to believe, for instance, that the small groups of early farmers could have made drastic inroads on the elm population. It is also extraordinary that the 'elm decline' does not seem to coincide with the arrival of Neolithic farmers – it is merely one factor in a series of vegetation changes that took

23 These leaf-shaped flint arrowheads are typical of those used by the first Neolithic farmers in Britain, and are very finely worked. They were found in Co. Antrim

0   1   2   3   4 cm

place around this time. Furthermore it is now believed that Mesolithic people cleared forest to facilitate the herding of animals, so the change from forest to open land does not necessarily denote the arrival of agriculturalists proper.

Extensive continental research has suggested that the adoption of farming was not the outcome of a rapid 'revolution' but can be traced through a pattern of gradual changes in the environment. In the first phase an increase in bracken and sedges and a decline in elm pollen suggests human activity (either Mesolithic or Neolithic) by pioneer groups. This was followed by a phase of vigorous forest clearance during which elm declined rapidly and grasses and weeds such as nettles became more common. In a third phase, as fields were worked, plantain and other weeds of cultivation became common in the pollen record. Then as the soil became exhausted, fields were abandoned and regeneration took place. This classic pattern has been observed on a number of sites, notably at Fallahogy in Co. Londonderry in Ireland, where the radio-carbon dates start the story before 4000 BC.

The same pattern can be seen in Britain. At Barfield Tarn, in the Lake District of Cumbria, an elm decline was accompanied by the increase of plantain and other weeds of cultivation. Elm then recovered and the weeds died out, suggesting temporary regeneration. This was followed by another decline in elm and other trees (notably oak) and the appearance of cereals. So vigorous was the cultivation, that erosion of the soil resulted.

The picture that emerges, then, is that during the second half of the fifth millennium BC, small groups of farmers settled in northern and eastern Ireland, Cumbria and southern England. It was either these settlers or contemporary Mesolithic herdsmen who first went out of an early morning with their axes poised over their shoulders and came back with blunt blades and large tracts of land cleared. Once this pioneering had been completed, it was but a short step to cultivating the land, to establishing lines of trade and communication and eventually, to building what are the earliest Neolithic monuments that have survived.

How easy was it to clear forest with stone axes? Many experiments have been carried out using stone axes, and the general conclusion has been that on softwoods they were virtually as effective as steel implements. In Denmark an experiment in 1954 indicated that 500 square metres of forest could be cleared by three men in four hours (or, in more likely terms, one man could have cleared a hectare in five weeks). The experiment used flint axes which were hafted in accordance with Neolithic custom. The trees were cut at knee height, the axe held at about 50 degrees to the tree trunk, in order to chip off long pieces. When felled, the trunk of the tree resembled a sharpened pencil. The Danes found that the average tree took about 30 minutes to fell, but more recent experiments in Czechoslovakia clocked only 7 minutes for a smallish tree. Massive trees could be brought down by girding them and leaving them to die.

There can be little doubt that Neolithic farmers made a considerable impact on the landscape of Britain. As might be expected, the lands favoured seem to have been light, well-drained soils (the sands and gravels, the chalk and the younger limestones). In these areas farmers established themselves in sufficient numbers to open the land permanently without any subsequent regeneration. The chalk downlands of Wiltshire, for instance, were forest until cleared for ever by Neolithic man. The breckland of East Anglia and the coastal plain of south-west Cumbria were permanently cleared too. Other parts of the country such as the Thames valley around Oxford and Strathtay in Perthshire may have been subjected to the same treatment. Although the land was used for both pasture and tillage, on the Wessex chalk farming was predominantly pastoral, and it was the constant cropping of the fields by sheep and goats that prevented regeneration from taking place.

During the Neolithic there were some changes in the overall pattern of farming, pastoralism perhaps increasing as time went on. Around 3700 BC anyone who happened to be passing in the neighbourhood of Windmill Hill, a meeting-place near Avebury in Wiltshire, would have heard mostly the sound of cattle lowing. The ratio of cattle to sheep and goats to pigs was 66:12:16 (it is a popular archaeological joke, as well as being a truism that you can't often tell the sheep from the goats, from the surviving remains). By 3400 BC the ratio had changed to 60:25:15, the increase in sheep and goats perhaps being due to the increase in grassland.

When a Neolithic farmer walked his newly prepared fields in spring, he sowed predominantly wheat (emmer with some einkorn). Archaeologists know the proportion of crops grown from the subtle evidence of the grain impressions on pots. Those from Windmill Hill showed only 10 per cent that were not of wheat and most of this small minority were impressions of barley. Spelt may have been grown, but it seems to have been very rare. Hunting was of minimal importance among the early Neolithic communities, though Neolithic hosts were apparently able to offer apples and nuts to their guests and families.

```
0    1    2    3    4    5 cm
L____|____|____|____|____|
```

Dogs warmed the feet of Neolithic farmers – a complete canine skeleton was among the finds from Windmill Hill, as well as parts of those of two puppies. They were of a breed similar to a fox terrier, known as a turbary dog. It will surprise nobody to learn that they were fed on bones – so rich in calcium was the excrement that it has survived in the ditches of Windmill Hill in its original state.

24   With only flint at their disposal, the Neolithic inhabitants of Britain could produce a variety of useful tools. These were all found at Southacre, Norfolk, and consist of (*top to bottom*) an arrowhead, spokeshave, handled scraper, spearhead and burin

25 (a) The tools of the flint-worker's trade. At the top (*left*) can be seen a flint hammer-stone, with next to it an un-finished arrowhead. Below are (*left*) a 'fabricator', possibly for fine flaking, and (*right*) a core of flint of tortoise shape, left after flakes had been detached. All from Windmill Hill, Wiltshire

25 (b) Typical late Neolithic transverse or *petit tranchet* arrowheads from Windmill Hill, Wilts. These were used in the later Neolithic, perhaps for game

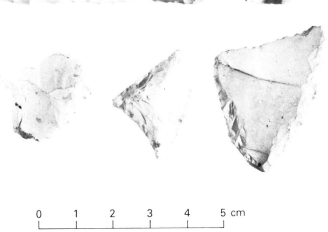

```
0    1    2    3    4    5 cm
```

It would at first seem far-fetched to hope to discover the farming methods of Neolithic man, but a remarkable field was found sealed beneath an earthen long barrow at South Street, Wiltshire. It displayed criss-cross marks made by the plough as it cut into the subsoil. Such 'cross-ploughing' (with the furrows at right-angles to each other) was first used to break up the ground and thereafter cultivation took place with hoes and spades. Neolithic workers may have demarcated fields by walls which they built by throwing out the stones in clearance banks; field walls of the period are known from several sites in Ireland. Although no fields as early as that at South Street have been authenticated else-where in Britain, there are several groups of small irregular fields bounded by curvilinear walls and associated with huts which are presumed to belong to the late Neolithic and Bronze Ages. Many of these are to be seen in Devon and Cornwall, notably on Dartmoor.

It is in Shetland, however, that fields can be associated with undoubtedly Neolithic settlements, albeit of a late date. Here the fields are demarcated by stone dykes, and extend from between 18.3 and 29.3 metres in width. Clearance banks of stones are found adjacent (p. 106). The inhabitants of each dwelling apparently farmed up to six fields.

The grain was harvested with flint sickles, and ground in saucer-querns with a circular motion – later saddle-querns (which were ground with a backwards and forwards motion) became popular. Pottery spoons may have been used to scrape the flour off the quern.

Animals appear to have been butchered on the spot. There is no real evidence for autumn slaughter, in order to reduce the fodder requirement over winter, as was common in later periods.

Of the domestic crafts practised, flint-working was of course important, for where the stone was available most tools were manufactured out of it. Bone provided the material for a wide variety of tools. Antler combs were made to scrape the loose hair from skins, points were made for piercing skins and an assortment of other tools such as pins, antler mattocks, deer antler picks, shoulder-blade shovels and miscellanea such as pendants for personal ornament have been found. Wedges and chisels were also fashioned. It is unknown whether cloth was woven before the late Neolithic, though flax was certainly grown and a spindle whorl was discovered at Durrington Walls, Wiltshire. The sheep that were domesticated may have been kept as much for their fleeces as for their meat. Potters worked both for the local market and for trade – much of their wares imitated leather or basketry vessels. Thus can it be deduced that leather and basketry containers existed, though none have survived.

Wood must have been used for a wide variety of tools which have perished. An early Neolithic site at Ehenside Tarn, Cumbria, has yielded an assortment of wooden objects. The settlement came to light in the 1870s, when a small lake was being drained. The inhabitants used wooden bowls (of which one fragment survived), leisters (fish-spears) and clubs. Of the two axe-hafts found, one contained a polished stone axe. A dug-out canoe with its associated paddle serves as a reminder that in the absence of wheeled vehicles men in the Stone Age had to resort to more energetic methods of transporting goods or passengers. There is evidence, for example, for the use of sledges during the Neolithic and the harvest was brought in by this method in the Scottish borders even into the twentieth century. One piece of wood from Ehenside Tarn was decorated with a reticulated pattern.

A fragment of a wooden bowl turned up at Storrs Moss in Lancashire, while more recently a range of Neolithic wood-work has come to light during the excavation of the Sweet Track in the Somerset Levels. The prize of the collection there was an oak vessel rather reminiscent of a modern butter dish. Two spatulas (for stirring porridge?) were also found, one near a pottery vessel. Most of the objects were pointed tools, awls, pins and the like, but there were a few toggles (perhaps for clothing), the tip of a longbow, a complete hazel-wood bow, a holly-wood club or mattock, the end of a wooden spear and a knife. Two arrowshafts were complete with their leaf-shaped flint arrowheads. A rope made from twisted grass was used by someone to tie up a boat or tether an animal in about 4000 BC, to judge by radio-carbon dates.

Much more advanced than the Sweet Track bows are those found at Meare and Ashcott in the Somerset Levels in 1961. Radio-carbon dates indicate that these were used around 3400 BC. Both were virtually as tall as a man and the Meare bow elaborately bound with cross-webbing between bands of binding. This was probably to compensate for the bow's thinness. A reproduction of one of the bows was tried out, and found to hit its target from a range of sixty yards.

Trade and industry
Nobody interested in early Britain should omit to descend to the bottom of a chalk-cut shaft and peer along the narrow galleries running off it at Grimes Graves in Norfolk, not far from Brandon, where until recently skilled flint knappers fashioned gun-flints from the same seam as those delved out by Neolithic miners. Here is one of the few places in Britain where it is possible to gain for a moment some impression of what life must have been like four or five thousand years ago. Although the character of Thetford Forest is somewhat different from the virgin woodland that confronted Neolithic man, nevertheless its extent serves as a reminder that the habitations and industries of Neolithic man must have been similarly tucked away in clearings and woods. The Neolithic flint mines lie in an area of open

heathland, pitted like a lunar landscape with the hollows of infilled mine shafts.

Grimes Graves made a notable impact on that indefatigable Victorian antiquary, Canon Greenwell. He was here in 1870 and wrote acidly of one shaft, 'Here I am with that accursed pit, which is doubtless the original bottomless one.'

The flint mines at Grimes Graves were worked in the late Neolithic, and have mostly been dated by radio-carbon to

the period between 2500 BC and 2200 BC. The pottery associated was of a type known as Grooved ware, which is found in late Neolithic henge sites (p. 114). No fewer than 300 pits are recorded in the 35 acre (15ha) site. The miners sank a shaft up to 12m deep through the chalk to reach good seams of tabular flint. Galleries were run off the main shaft to exploit the seams. As each shaft was worked out the debris from the next one was dumped in it. The miners climbed down into the pit either by steps cut into the side of the chalk or by ladders. In one of the pits skeletons of voles were found at the bottom along with the gnawed remains of antlers. Had the little creatures fallen in from the top they would have been killed instantly, so it can be inferred that they arrived there by means of ladders or ropes. The galleries were lit artificially by lamps made from hollowed lumps of chalk. After excavation the sooty stains from the

26 Hollows in the brecklands of Norfolk at Grimes Graves betray the presence of the shafts of Neolithic flint mines. The dog is sitting in the centre of one shaft. The mines cover an area of 15 ha in extent

27 At the bottom of the main shaft the miners at Grimes Graves, Norfolk, drove galleries along to follow the seam of flint which was required for Neolithic axes. Flints can be seen in a band half-way between the top of the picture and the top of the galleries

ancient lights could be seen on the roofs of the galleries. Heaps of charcoal have also been found in the galleries where burnt-out torches were discarded. Although hearths and domestic refuse have been found in the partly filled-in shafts, no domestic rubbish has come from the galleries. This worried early explorers, who came to the conclusion that the miners 'quitted the shafts at meal-times'!

The shafts and galleries were dug out using antler picks and shovels made from animal shoulder-blades. Scratches on the walls of the shafts were possibly the work of bored miners, and a drawing on a stone of an elk or a red deer has been found on the site. One antler pick eerily still retained a chalky fingerprint from its ancient user. There are a few marks made by stone axes on the sides of the shafts which remind one of what life was like for the miners.

The most remarkable discovery at Grimes Graves, however, was an abandoned shaft that had been converted to a shrine. This particular tunnel had not hit the flint seam and was abandoned as a viable mine at an early stage. When the miners left, a figurine of a goddess, fat and fecund, was carved out of chalk and placed on a ledge with an adjacent chalk phallus. Around both the ancients had piled antler picks. It does not take a great flight of fancy to picture what happened here – the miners, disappointed at their failure in locating the flint, made an offering to propitiate their goddess. But this reconstruction may well be too imaginative. Doubt has been cast on the antiquity of the 'shrine', leaving us as perplexed as ever.

Once mined, the flint was fashioned into chipped stone axes and traded from the mines. Grimes Graves is not unique – other flint mines are known, notably at Cissbury, Harrow Hill and Blackpatch, all in Sussex. Cissbury holds a

28 This chalk figurine of a fertility goddess is unique in Neolithic Britain. It was offered by the miners at Grimes Graves, Norfolk, when a particular mine shaft proved unrewarding

particular fascination since it was investigated by Pitt-Rivers in the 1860s and 1870s. One of the Cissbury shafts was no less than 12.8 m deep. Drama accompanied the excavations – while crawling along a gallery he came to the bottom of another shaft which was infilled with blocks of chalk. As he attempted to pull these away 'presently a well-formed and perfect human jaw fell down from above, and on looking up we could perceive the remainder of the skull fixed with the base downwards and the face towards the west, between two pieces of chalk rubble.' The skull belonged to a young woman who had either fallen head-first into the shaft, or whose body had been unceremoniously thrown into it.

It was while investigating the Cissbury shafts that Pitt-Rivers pioneered experimental archaeology. He was curious to find out how easy it was to dig out a flint mine with antler picks and shoulder-blade shovels. Being a military man and

29 Flint miners' tools. The antler pick is from Grimes Graves, the shoulder-blade shovel from Cissbury, as is the antler 'wedge' and rough-out for an axe beneath it. The two chalk miner's lamps at the bottom left come from Cissbury and Grimes Graves respectively

a believer in not asking the men to do anything you would not do yourself, he and another man dug out a cubic yard of mine with picks, wedges and punches fashioned from a pair of antlers. It took one-and-a-half-hours, from which he deduced that a mine gallery might have been dug out in twelve hours. He used ox scapula shovels to load his wheelbarrow, but came to the conclusion that it was less efficient than using bare hands, though it left the person doing the removal in better shape! A similar experiment carried out by Dr E. C. Curwen in 1926 came to the conclusion that using the scapula it took four times as long to load a wheelbarrow as using an army spade, and slightly longer than using bare hands!

Axes of good stone were at a premium in Neolithic society, and outside the flint areas other types of stone were mined or quarried to make rough axes which were then traded far and wide. A number of important 'axe factories' have been identified in Britain and Ireland. The most famous were at Great Langdale (Cumbria), Graig Lwyd (Penmaenmawr, Clwyd), Mynydd Rhiw (Gwynedd) and Tievebulliagh (Antrim). Most suitable were the tough, fine-grained igneous or metamorphic stones which could be

30 Rough-out for flint axe (*bottom*) and axe broken in polishing (*top*) from Cissbury, Sussex

0 1 2 3 4 5 cm

given a sharp edge. Usually, as at Great Langdale, the material was obtained from a scree, and roughly worked on the spot. The cave used by the Langdale axe-makers still exists next to its scree, which contains large proportions of their waste material.

Occasionally shafts were dug to obtain suitable stone – this happened at Mynydd Rhiw. The site of this axe factory, high up in the Lleyn peninsula, is today remote from any habitation. The Mynydd Rhiw miners were very choosy about the stone they required. On this mountain an igneous intrusion of dolerite had forced its way between the bedding places of shale, and the heat had transformed the shale into an extremely hard metamorphic rock, which, like flint,

91

fractured conchoidally. The miners ignored the shale and dolerite, though the latter was used in other areas for axes.

Extensive trade links were built up from the axe factories. Hitherto unknown factories and products are constantly being discovered, and the extent to which axes changed hands is remarkable. Tievebulliagh axes were taken northwards to Aberdeenshire and even Shetland, and south to Kent and Devon. Axes from Graig Lwyd reached West Lothian, Yorkshire, East Anglia and Dorset. Great Langdale

31 These superb jade axes were probably imported from the Continent and attest far-flung trade links in Neolithic Britain. Both were found at Cunzierton, Roxburghshire, Scotland. Length: 19.1 cm and 17.8 cm

axes reached Cornwall in the south and Aberdeenshire in the north. This was not a case of the occasional axe ending up far from its place of origin – often dozens of products from one particular factory have been found in one specific region hundreds of miles away.

Radio-carbon dating has shown that the axe industry was established at an early date. The first 'factories' to have been in operation appear to have been those of Cornwall, which were trading from before 4000 BC, around the same time that the Sussex flint mines were beginning to be worked.

The pottery trade
Pottery production boomed in the Neolithic, with pots being transported over surprising distances. One of the key areas

32 This finely finished Neolithic bowl from Windmill Hill, Wilts., is typical of some of the better-quality pottery which is found in south-west England in the early Neolithic. It is datable to around 4000 BC

for the manufacture of ceramics was the Lizard peninsula of Cornwall. Here gabbroic clay was used for fine pots which found their way into homes in Cornwall, Devon and Wiltshire. Local potters imitated imported pots to cater for their markets. For instance, they tried to copy the smooth rounded pots which occasionally have lugs for suspension from a string. Pots with these characteristic features have been designated the Hembury style after a site in Devon where they were first recognized. Pots from the Bath/Frome area of Somerset reached Wiltshire. The trade in pottery was not short-lived: Cornish pottery was being produced for a wide market from around 4200 BC to around 3400 BC.

For the conduct of such a trade a considerable degree of organization was necessary, as well as good routes and transport. Canoes and probably more elaborate, custom-built craft were used for deliveries while overland some of the famous prehistoric trackways of southern England no doubt relate to the demands of markets in Neolithic times. Some tracks discovered in the Somerset Levels, such as the Sweet Track (p. 96), or the Chilton Tracks were indubitably first trudged by men laden with their wares in the Neolithic period.

The Sweet Track, the earliest so far discovered, displayed an advanced method of construction that must relate to its

33   This coarse and undecorated bowl with lug handles is typical of Early Neolithic Windmill Hill style ware, and probably imitates wood or leather. It is among the earliest pottery found in Britain. From a long barrow at Norton Bavant, Wilts. Such pots were widely traded in south-west England in the early Neolithic

34   This baggy bowl is typical of a type of Neolithic pottery known as Heslerton ware. It was found at Heslerton in the East Riding of Yorkshire, in a trench under a barrow

importance. Its foundation was a line of rails, pegged into the marsh with wooden pins. Upon this ancient engineers had laid a line of planks end to end, fastened into place by thin pegs driven through notches cut in the wood. Where the level was uneven, turf was used to build up the foundation. Oak, ash, elm, lime, alder, hazel and holly were utilized, though not all these woods flourished locally. At intervals of about 3 to 5 metres tall posts were driven into the marsh to mark the line of the track. These may have served a similar purpose to modern cat's-eyes – perhaps they helped travellers to follow the route when it was finished. The Sweet Track and several others in the Somerset Levels were

35 This bowl decorated with cord impressions to imitate basketry is typical of a series of different types of decorated late Neolithic pottery in Britain. Known collectively as Peterborough ware, this particular example of the Mortlake style came from Mortlake on the river Thames, and was associated with pieces of beaker belonging to the 'Copper Age'

obviously built to connect the scattered 'island' settlements in the marsh.

Later in the Neolithic period (c. 2940 BC) ancient road builders worked on the Walton Track. Discovered in 1975, this remarkable highway was built of hurdles which were laid on a particularly wet stretch of marshland. The hurdles were just over a metre wide and between 2.50m and 3m long, and were woven of hazel with willow withies to bind the corners and edges together.

Settlements

A clear scenario of trade and industry in Neolithic Britain has thus emerged – but what of the home life of these miners and merchants?

Surviving houses and settlements of the Neolithic are relatively few in number. One of the earliest was excavated at Fengate near Peterborough in 1972, and dated to 3700 BC or somewhat later. This rectangular post-built structure had daubed walls, and measured 8.50m by 7m. Its occupants were clearly farmers, for two fragments of flint sickles with silica lustre were found in the hut, along with early Neolithic pottery.

Such simple rectangular timber huts are known from a number of sites, of which the best known are Clegyr Boia, in Pembrokeshire, and Haldon Hill, Devon. The Haldon house measured a roomy 7.6m by 4.9m, with sturdy stone foundations to hold the timber uprights. Two post-holes on the

36 The Sweet Track, a Neolithic trackway through the Somerset Levels, the earliest road so far discovered in Britain. The picture shows its foundation of rails, driven into the marsh with wooden pins. On this planks were laid end to end, fastened by pegs driven through notches cut in the wood

central axis indicate that it had a gabled roof. The entrance was in one corner of the building. At Clegyr Boia varied tastes or functions were reflected, as one hut was circular, and another was a rectangle. The latter measured 7.3m by 3.7m, and was built into an angle of rock outcrop with eight posts in two rows. However, most of the evidence for early Neolithic settlement takes the form of storage pits which are associated with random groups of post-holes and sometimes gullies or ditches.

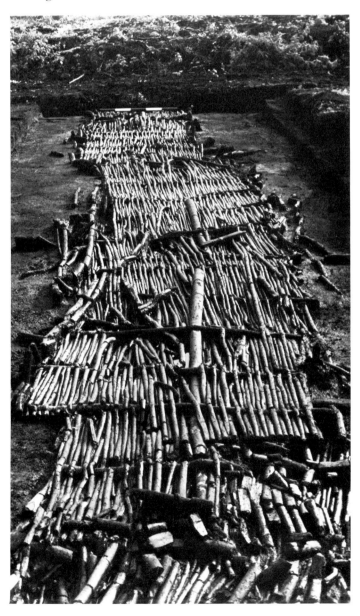

37 Neolithic hurdles found during excavation of the Walton Track, one of the roads through the Somerset Levels. These were laid around 2940 BC on a particularly wet stretch of marshland. They are made of hazel and willow withies, the latter used to bind the corners and edges together

The householder at Clegyr Boia lived in an establishment very similar to one on the hilltop settlement at Carn Brea in Cornwall. The site, which is well worth visiting, chronicles the span of early British history. Apart from its Neolithic remains, it has yielded a fine hoard of late Bronze Age axes, two hoards of Celtic gold coins, Roman coins, and a jumble of later finds. One of its three peaks is crowned by a medieval castle, another by a modern monument. Most of the visible remains belong to the Iron Age hill-fort, but Neolithic fortifications have been discovered on the eastern peak of the hill, where a massive dry-stone wall linked outcrops of granite, so that the hilltop was encircled. Various structures were sited on terraces within the hilltop enclosure – they included a lean-to house of Clegyr Boia style, 2.50m by 7m, its wall constructed of hurdling with a door at its southern end and a hearth in the interior. Pits inside the house were used for garbage disposal and as containers for storage pots. Eleven terraces are distinguishable, and excavation has suggested that most, if not all, had houses on them. This would imply a population of about 100 to 120 people at Carn Brea at any one time. This seems a reasonable estimate, in view of the manpower necessary to build the wall. Radio-carbon dates indicate that the people made their homes on this terraced hill around 3700 BC and that they toiled to build the stone wall later (but before 3500 BC).

There is growing evidence that aggression was commoner than prehistorians once supposed, and the fortifications at Carn Brea were not unique. On Broome Heath, Ditchingham, Norfolk, for instance, a C-shaped Neolithic enclosure was furnished with a double bank and ditch, the inner bank of which had been revetted in front with a line of linked stakes and which had been crowned by a fence. At Lyles Hill in Co. Antrim a single bank surrounded the hilltop, and a late Neolithic enclosure at Waulud's Bank, Bedfordshire, seems to have been defensive – its single bank and ditch enclosed an oval of about 18 acres. Broome Heath has been dated by radio-carbon to shortly after 3000 BC.

Murder and warfare are perhaps attested by two recent finds. Excavations in 1978 at Crickley Hill, Gloucestershire, have produced evidence that a Neolithic siege took place – arrowheads were strewn along the line of the defences. In 1975 excavations at Fengate, Peterborough, brought to light a bizarre burial. Deposited in an unmarked, roughly dug grave were the skeletons of four individuals, an adult male of about 25–30, a female of about the same age, a child of uncertain sex but aged about 8–12, and an infant of about

3–4; in other words, what would appear to be a family group. The man, however, had a flint arrowhead lodged between the eighth and ninth ribs of his body. Its tip was missing. Had this inflicted a fatal wound, and were he and his family the victims of some guerrilla attack? If so, and it seems very likely, they are the earliest known murder victims in Britain.

Even as this book was being written, evidence was coming to light that the chiefs of early Neolithic Britain were living in a fashion not unlike the chiefs of the Dark Ages over four millennia later. At Balbridie in Grampian excavations brought to light in 1977 the remains of a timber hall, 26m by 13m, with bowed-out double end walls and with three internal divisions. At first believed to be of Dark Age date, radio-carbon testing of wood from several post-holes indicated that the hall was built between 4000 and 3500 BC. Sherds of 'Unstan' pottery were found in a post-hole, providing corroboration for the radio-carbon date.

Skara Brae and Rinyo

In late Neolithic Britain there were economic and social changes accompanied by an upsurge in religious zeal. For instance, there were signs that due to intensive cultivation the soil in some areas became exhausted, and regeneration took place. The increase in pigs around this time may be connected with the expanding forest areas which gradually

38 Skara Brae, Orkney, a late Neolithic village of stone-built huts. In the foreground can be seen the shell midden and behind can be seen the beds and central hearth in a house. Shortage of wood resulted in even furniture being made of stone, and the village owes its preservation to being engulfed by sand

encroached upon old farm land. Transverse arrowheads (those with a broad cutting edge rather than a sharp point) became common, and these were almost certainly designed for the hunting of wild-fowl. Pastoralism also increased. Some prehistorians believe that these economic changes went hand-in-hand with social ones. Up until this time there is evidence that people lived in medium-sized tribal groups of fairly equal status that collaborated with one another for undertakings that required communal effort. In late Neolithic and early Bronze Age Britain there are signs that chiefdoms were emerging – chiefdoms that were able to expand, on the strength of their trade and resources, at the expense of the less fortunate. Apparently powerful leaders organized the people into the creation of amazing works of communal effort. Hitherto such feats had been beyond the capabilities of the tribal group of 25–50 individuals that have been estimated as collaborating with their neighbours in the building of earlier ritual monuments of the fourth millennium BC.

These chiefs may have been secular leaders or priest-kings (p. 115) but discoveries in the Northern Isles of Scotland have brought their homes and lifestyles into brilliant focus. Although the chiefdoms of northern Scotland may seem a far cry from those of Wessex or Yorkshire, and although it is obvious that life in Orkney was not the same as that in Wessex, nevertheless it is clear that

39 Interior of house 7, Skara Brae, the best preserved of the houses in this village. Notice the stone boxes set into the floor and the rubbing stone next to the 'dresser' as well as the cupboards in the walls

all over late Neolithic Britain societies shared much in common. Archaeologically these late Neolithic communities are most readily recognized by their highly ornamented pottery, which is called Grooved ware on account of its incised ornament. Wherever it is found it probably heralds people with other characteristics in common. More cumbersome is the term 'Rinyo-Clacton culture' which has also been used to describe the same phenomenon, after one Orcadian and one Essex site where the pottery was first recognized.

Grooved ware came into fashion around 3000 BC. The earliest of the Orcadian sites pre-dates this. Indeed, the Knap O' Howar is older than any other standing house in north-west Europe. Lying on a sandy shoreline on the remote island of Papa Westray, the site is idyllically peaceful. Here the visitor can admire two approximately rectangular houses, which inter-connect. The larger is about 9.5m by 4.8m, the smaller 7.8m by 3.4m. Stone projecting slabs separate the interior into two rooms in the case of the larger house, three in the case of the smaller. They were probably roofed with timber and turf, and had an entrance passage at the north-west end, checked for a door. The housewife of five thousand years ago obviously demanded and obtained built-in cupboards in the smaller building. A midden of food refuse mostly composed of shells surrounded and underlay the houses. The Knap O' Howar occupants seem to have grown grain, to judge by the querns found. Radio-carbon dates for the site range between 3700 and 3100 BC. Pottery from the site was of Unstan type, the precursor of Grooved ware.

The Orcadian villages of Skara Brae and Rinyo are somewhat more advanced, though only the former is well preserved. Recently a third village has been rediscovered at the Links of Noltland on Westray. It is probably at least four times as large as Skara Brae itself.

Skara Brae is one of the most remarkable prehistoric sites in Europe: a Neolithic 'Pompeii'. It was kept intact by a sandstorm that buried it nearly three thousand years ago. So well preserved is it that for a long time archaeologists refused to believe it was as ancient as has now been proved. Due to the dearth of wood, the builders used the local and more durable flagstone for everything, including the furniture, which has in consequence survived.

Skara Brae first came to antiquaries' attention in the 1850s, when a storm partly exposed some of the houses, which were uncovered in a haphazard fashion during the next ten years. In 1913 it happened by chance that Professor Boyd

Dawkins, the famous cave explorer (p. 44) was visiting the owner of the site, Balfour-Stewart, and heard of the village. He and some other house-guests began serious digging, and as a result Skara Brae became the focus of scholarly interest. In 1924 the site was taken over by the then Office of Works, and in the same year a storm washed away most of one of the houses. Professor Childe was called in to supervise the clearance of the dwellings and passages prior to their consolidation for the public, though because of the

40 View into one of the houses at Skara Brae, through the entrance leading from the main passage-way or 'street' of the village. A dresser can be seen against the back wall

need for display extensive archaeological excavation was impossible.

Despite his vast knowledge, Childe did not believe that he was excavating a Neolithic village. He though it was 'Pictish' and datable to about 500 BC (the Picts are now known to have lived nearly a millennium later). Nevertheless he was amazed at his findings. Many years later his landlady reported that Childe never seemed to eat during the excavations – when finds were rich he was too excited and when a rare day produced no finds, he was too depressed. Eventually, however, Childe was the first to recognize the real age of Skara Brae. He was called in to excavate the similar site of Rinyo which produced a fragment of Beaker pottery (p. 142). Both sites were thus proved to be at least as early as the end of the Neolithic.

The builders of both Skara Brae and Rinyo went home at the end of the day to houses that were about 4.6m to 6.1m across, entered through a single doorway. The weather was excluded by a wooden door, as shown by the elaborate bar-holes, and sometimes the houses even had intra-mural 'guard chambers'. The centre of each house was cheered and warmed by a hearth on which peat burned, and belongings would have been arranged on the stone dresser that stood against the rear wall. Each night the householders would have flopped down into their fixed beds, formed with three slabs which kept the bedding in place and no doubt also warded off draughts. Similar box beds could be seen in the Hebrides until recently. Another feature recalling the recent Hebrides was the placing of a larger bed on the right-hand side of the entrance, presumably for the master of the house, his wife having to content herself with a smaller 'box' on the left-hand side as the house was entered. Above each bed was a handy shelf for possessions. Clay-luted boxes set in the floor probably kept fish-bait alive. Such built-in stone furniture long remained fashionable in Orkney and can still be seen today. If they lay abed unable to sleep, the inhabitants of the Neolithic houses would have been able to trace the lines of the corbelled walls which sloped inwards about 2.4 or 3.1m above the floor. Between them and the night sky were whalebone or driftwood rafters, which carried turf or stone roofing.

In all, the village comprised about six houses, leading off a covered alley. The entire settlement was covered with a midden of peat-ash, dung and broken bones which filled the spaces between the houses and rose above them to a height of about 2.4m, only the roofs projecting above the giant rubbish tip. It kept out the cold northern winds, and was probably more effective than cavity-wall insulation, as well as obviating the need for garbage disposal operatives. Another 'modern' feature of the village was its drainage system. A sewer ran under the village, reached by 'inspection chambers'.

In 1972–3 further excavations were carried out at Skara Brae, which provided additional information about the way of life of the inhabitants. Radio-carbon dates obtained showed that it had been occupied from around 3100 BC to around 2500 BC.

The inhabitants were, like the Beaker people (see p. 141), mainly cattle men, though as time went on sheep and goats were more important and pigs were kept in small numbers. Dogs were kept as pets or to protect the livestock. The villagers took advantage of their coastal situation to fish – mainly for bottom-feeders such as cod and coalfish. The excavator of the site has suggested that the stone tanks in the houses may have been intended to contain limpets for bait rather than eating. These gasteropod molluscs have been regarded as a food supply only in times of famine in northern Scotland. In 1814 Sir Walter Scott noted in his diary while visiting the Northern Isles that 'the rest of the inhabitants of the Orcades despise those of Swona because they eat limpets, as being the last of human meannesses.'

The finds made in 1972–3 included part of a wooden handle, and several pieces of leather rope, similar to those made in the north and west of Scotland until recent times and used for tying thatch on the roofs of houses. At Skara Brae they were probably used for tethering animals.

The most intriguing finds, however, were ten puff-balls. They were not intended for eating since they were all adult fruit, but may have been collected for medicinal purposes. They have been used in the more recent past to staunch bleeding and to aid the clotting of blood in small wounds.

Numerous pieces of pumice came to light that had probably been brought by the tides from Iceland. They were probably used for shaping the rich array of bone tools from the village. Some limpet shells had been used as containers for ochre, perhaps used as 'make-up' or simply as paint – whalebone dishes filled with pigment were found in the original excavations.

Skara Brae has other puzzles. In Hut 7 Childe uncovered a slab with curious incised marks cut along its edge that looked uncommonly like runic writing. Other geometric designs can be seen on stones in the main passage. Are they merely ornamental? Are they magical signs? Or are they an attempt at writing? Until recently the last suggestion would

41 Sherds of pottery from Skara Brae, Orkney, decorated with applied and incised ornament. This type of pottery is usually termed 'Grooved ware' and was formerly known as 'Rinyo-Clacton' after a site in Orkney and one in Essex. Note the elaborate design of the sherd at the bottom right, with double spiral and double lozenge, perhaps due to Irish influence

have seemed preposterous, for it was universally agreed that writing had been developed in the Near East and disseminated thence. However, recent research in the Balkans has brought to light the famous Tartaria tablets.

42 The entrance stone to the chambered tomb of Newgrange, Co. Meath, Ireland. Compare the ornament on this stone with the sherd illustrated bottom right in plate 41

These turned up in a Neolithic tell and appear to be the result of an independent invention of writing there, an art which was subsequently forgotten. If it is a little far-fetched to regard the Skara Brae carvings as genuine writing, there is a case for thinking them symbolic 'ideograms' which had a specific meaning for their engravers.

Also puzzling among the finds from Skara Brae was a carved stone ball. Of unknown function, similar orbs have been discovered in northern Scotland, and from their spiral ornament it has been deduced that their makers had connections with the Boyne valley of Ireland where a similar art is found. Some were beautifully carved. But what were they? One dramatic suggestion is that they were for *bolas* – these were connected to ropes and thrown at animals to entangle their legs and bring them down. Another suggestion is that they were used in a game – could the popularity of bowls in modern Scotland be due to such an ancient origin for the game?

Houses and farms in Shetland

Around the time that Skara Brae and Rinyo were desirable residential areas, other late Neolithic farmers were tilling the rocky soil of Shetland. Today the remains of their homes are dotted over a barren landscape. The scattered grey stones of the foundations and walls of their fields blend in with the heather. None is more desolate than Stanydale. The un-fenced road cuts through the Shetland moorland, until a signpost apparently pointing towards nowhere directs mystified wanderers to the 'temple'. Marker posts lead the follower on like a Will o' the Wisp across the flat heather, through which tiny brown rivulets of peat-stained water flow. Then, when it seems as though the moor is going to continue for eternity, the ruined foundations of a building confirm the fact that humans have been this way before. Many mistake this for the 'temple'. In fact they are the foundations of a Neolithic house – the 'temple' with its similar plan lies further afield yet in this wilderness.

The Stanydale house is typical of Shetland Neolithic habitations. Here the farmers favoured approximately oval homes, with a main chamber from which opened one or two side cells or recesses. These recall the compartments of a chambered tomb. They are carefully built, great skill being displayed in the way in which amorphous blocks of stone have been manouvered into place. There are over 70 such crofters' houses. Often the houses were isolated, but some are clustered together in groups of three or four. Beyond, the irregular-shaped fields are edged with stone dykes and measure between 18.3m and 79.3m at their greatest extent. Here and there are clearance heaps of stones gathered off the fields, and now and again too are found the burnt mounds of stone that probably mark communal cooking places.

The Stanydale 'temple' is similar in layout to the houses, but much more substantial. In shape, however, it is more like the heel cairns, the Shetland variety of 'chambered tombs'. Its central chamber measures 11.9m by 6.7m, and excavation showed that its roof was supported by two spruce posts. Spruce was not native to Shetland, and the timber must have reached the island by drifting from America.

Many people have compared the Stanydale building with the temples of Neolithic Malta. The similarity is probably fortuitous, as the great days of Maltese temple-building were long before Stanydale was conceived. On Whalsay a related site known as the Benie Hoose has been interpreted as the residence of priests who officiated at the temple about 100m away. The Benie Hoose and its temple had horned forecourts, which positively invites theories that ceremonies were performed there.

43 The Stanydale 'temple', Shetland. This remarkable late Neolithic structure shares some features in common with the Neolithic house sites of Shetland, but is appreciably larger. It was roofed, the supports being of spruce, a type of tree not native to Scotland which must have drifted from America. The temple also shares some features in common with the local type of Neolithic chambered tomb, the heel cairn

Fascinating though the Neolithic settlements of the Northern Isles are, in some measure they belong to another world. This is a fringe zone bordering on the great 'Circumpolar Province' which has its own tenacious tradition that seems to last unchanged from the upper Palaeolithic through to historical times. They serve, however, to illustrate the great variety of landscapes that could have been observed by any assiduous and curious traveller in Neolithic and early Bronze Age Britain.

Neolithic Man and the gods

Among the most remarkable Neolithic finds in Britain in recent years is a wooden effigy. Discovered in the Somerset Levels during the excavation of one of the trackways known as the Bell Track, it is carved out of ash wood and is hermaphroditic, with pronounced breasts and phallus. It had been used, upside down, in a peg and stick setting. Could it have been a votive offering intended to ensure the success of the track, or was it simply a small carving with little significance to the users that had been utilized in the construction of the track? Its discoverer, Dr John Coles, described it as a 'god dolly', and pointed out that such objects, which were of greater importance than dolls but hardly idols, have been carved in recent times. It was datable by radio-carbon to around 3000 BC or slightly later.

In Neolithic times, possibly more so than today, the world was a mysterious place fraught with constant danger. Disease might spread through a family for no apparent reason, animals could trample down fields and kill children. Storms could flatten the crops, start forest fires. Water supplies could dry up. Domesticated animals could die, milk-providers go dry. In a world in which humans were few and nature as yet largely untamed, every precaution had to be taken to keep the gods happy.

Prehistoric religion was not highly organized, with a pantheon of gods each with their own attributes. It is most unlikely that the inhabitants of prehistoric Britain were the adherents of a particular faith or series of faiths. Religion was much the same as superstition – a person did this or that because everyone had always done this or that to make sure that bad luck did not follow. Most superstition probably concerned the basic issues of human existence; death, birth and the maintenance of the food supply. Now and again archaeologists bring to light ritual carvings of 'goddesses' or 'gods' such as that found in the Bell Track or that from Grimes Graves. Whether these were the specific deities that were worshipped, or simply personifications of more abstract ideas such as fertility, we can but guess. Almost certainly prehistoric man was concerned with appeasing not one or two gods, but a myriad of deities who resided in each tree, river, hill or valley that was a part of his daily experience.

Religious observance was almost certainly not divorced from everyday secular life. Just as some people today might throw salt over their shoulders when they inadvertently upset the cellar, so did Neolithic Man probably appease the

44 God dolly, found in the make-up of the Bell Track, one of the Neolithic trackways of the Somerset Levels. Carved of ash, it is hermaphroditic. It has been dated to c.3000 BC, and sheds light on one aspect of Neolithic superstition – it may have been deliberately buried in a ritual connected with the laying of the track

spirits. Where religious observance required communal participation, it was in all probability attendant on other events – a local festival to celebrate the gathering-in of the harvest, a market or a feast to usher in spring. Accumulating evidence points to a continuing religious tradition in Britain. New superstitions were grafted to old. Ritual became more formalized, and became more tied up with what had recently been learned about the world.

Neolithic religion cannot therefore be isolated from what came afterwards in the Bronze Age. Ritual sites were in use in some cases for over a thousand years. As ritual became more formalized, sacred sites where pits had first been dug for offerings were enclosed by ditches and early enclosures became elaborated into more ambitious ritual centres. Experts stress that Stonehenge (which is datable to the Neolithic and Bronze Ages), is not a druid temple – the druids about whom classical authors wrote were a caste of Iron Age priests. But the druids were simply the last in a long tradition of priests and witch-doctors who fanned superstition and provided supernatural explanation for men's questions and fears.

To illustrate the longevity of religious traditions and the impossibility of assigning any one feature to particular periods, we need merely to consider one phenomenon that recurred in the Neolithic – the deposition of offerings, sometimes in pits. At Knockiveagh in Co. Down, for instance, beneath a tomb of later date excavators found the remains of ritual – pottery sherds mixed up with charcoal, cremated bone and pieces of stone axes were the vestiges of some early ceremony. Radio-carbon analysis assigned a date of *c*. 3700 BC to it.

There are signs that some middle Neolithic ritual sites in southern Britain were preceded by open shrines where pits were dug and offerings made. Windmill Hill, near Avebury in Wiltshire, was one such. In some places no further elaboration seems to have taken place – at South Cadbury (Somerset) pits had been in-filled almost as soon as they were dug – they contained such diversities as pottery, flint arrowheads, hazelnuts and a human jaw. Pits were still dug inside later ritual monuments, in some cases in a circle or set in lines. Many of these pits have been found to be nearly or totally devoid of any visible offerings. This has led to the suggestion that they could have contained timber posts or may have been marked in some way above ground, perhaps with a peg or a stone. If so, they could have been the precursors of the stone circles and alignments of standing stones of later prehistory. These putative posts may have been used for astronomical observations.

Ritual pits continued to be a feature of Bronze Age and even Iron Age customs. The strangest of all was the mysterious Wilsford shaft. Its discovery dates back to the summer of 1960, when archaeologists were investigating a prehistoric barrow at Normanton Gorse, Wiltshire. They noticed the weathered top of what looked like a very deep pit or well, and began to empty it.

It soon became apparent that the 'pit' was in fact a shaft which had silted up naturally. Roman and later pottery came from the top indicating that its construction must have been of greater antiquity. Finds of Iron Age pottery of the third century BC quite high up in the filling showed it to be older still. By the time winter had set in it was apparent to the excavators that another season of digging was necessary. Just before abandoning the shaft for the winter, at a depth of 12.2m, some pieces of middle Bronze Age pottery were encountered. The 1961 diggers were better equipped – an air supply (in case of concentrations of carbon dioxide), a telephone for communication with the surface, and artificial lighting were laid on, for nothing could be seen or heard at the bottom. A pump kept the shaft dry, and a mechanical hoist was used to carry spoil to the surface. By the end of 1961 a depth of over 24m had been reached, but not without difficulties. The shaft was water-logged, but yielded some worked wood, a shale ring and some more Bronze Age pottery.

The team was back in 1962. Communication with the surface this time was by means of closed-circuit television. The trip to the bottom of the shaft by now took 15 minutes. The bottom was reached 30.5m down, and had clearly been

45 Windmill Hill, Wiltshire, the most famous of the Neolithic causewayed camps in southern Britain, which has given its name to a phase of the early Neolithic. A ritual site, it seems to have been a communal meeting-place used sporadically for a variety of purposes. Note the Bronze Age round barrows and the crop-marks in the fields behind

unfinished. The walls showed the marks of antler picks, and a broad-bladed axe had also been used to trim back the sides. Where seams of flint had occurred, they had been neatly severed and trimmed. Among the debris at the bottom of the shaft were various wooden objects, such as parts of stave-built tubs, a hod and a bowl, as well as a length of rope and some ornate amber beads. Radio-carbon dating indicated that it had been dug around 1600 BC.

But how? It had clearly been dug in sections, but before each section was begun it had been checked with a template and plumb-bob, so that any mistake in alignment in the previous section was rectified in the next. There were no signs of footholds or places where beams had been fixed, and the only way that the spoil could have been removed was with the aid of winching gear.

A clue to the function of such a pit was its association with a burial site. Was it intended as a gate to the underworld? Another Bronze Age shaft at Swanwick in Hampshire had more grisly contents. The lower part of the shaft had walls coated with a rich brown substance. Once this had been flesh and blood. At the bottom a stake had been packed round with clay – for impaling victims perhaps? One thing is certain, however – these rituals represent traditions that started many centuries earlier.

Interrupted ditch enclosures

The earliest ritual monuments left by the Neolithic inhabitants of Britain are enclosures defined by ditches dug in sections with breaks or 'causeways'. They can be defined by a single circle of causewayed ditches, or by two or more concentric circles. For a long time they were believed to be settlements, and were given the name of 'causewayed camps'. The name has stuck, but excavations on a series of examples, notably the most famous causewayed camp of all, Windmill Hill in Wiltshire, have shown that they were not all places of habitation but sporadically used meeting-places. Forty-three examples are now known, scattered over the south and the Midlands. They were probably used for many purposes – from trading to sacrifices, from festivals to the ritual attendant on burial.

A curious feature of many causewayed camps is the number of polished stone axes that have been found in or near them. Could it be that they were a focus for axe trade? Axes themselves may have had some kind of symbolic importance in Neolithic ritual. Thirty-one axes have been found near Windmill Hill – these include examples from the main factories in Cornwall, Great Langdale, Tievebulliagh and Graig Lwyd. In this context the magnificent polished stone axes of jadeite that have been found all over Britain, from Cornwall to Caithness, assume a particular significance. Thin and very finely polished, they were clearly never used to chop down trees. They are also found on the Continent, especially in Brittany and along the Rhine, the distribution extending down to central Italy. Sometimes they have been found in hoards. The axes found in Britain were all imported from the Continent, but from where is not yet known for certain.

Although they are clearly not primarily intended for burials, a feature of several of the excavated causewayed camps are the burials found within them, usually deposited in the ditches. Could one of the functions of causewayed camps have been the laying out of the dead to decompose? Human bones scattered at a recently excavated site at Offham Hill in Sussex suggest this might have been the case, while at Hambledon Hill in Dorset deliberate deposits in the ditches contained fragments of human skulls which had clearly been put there without the rest of their bodies: other bones were rare, the commonest being long bones and fingers. Two infant burials were covered with a layer of stones – one had been buried wearing a necklace of three beads, the other was accompanied by two pieces of carved chalk. The interior of Hambledon was filled with pits, which seem to have been dug to receive different contents – some pits contained pottery of a type not found in the ditches, for instance. At Orsett, Essex, a timber palisade ran round the inside on the innermost ditch. At Freston, in Suffolk, aerial photography has revealed a building 36.6m by 9.1m long in the interior, with what seem to be 21 posts to each side and continuous sleeper trenches at the ends.

In a few cases ditched enclosures were converted into defensive structures. The workers at Crickley, Gloucestershire, for instance, built a bank faced with dry-stone walling inside the ditch, broken only by a narrow entrance and gate. At Hambledon outside the camp's main circle, cross-dykes were constructed in sections; beyond these an outwork was formed with a causewayed ditch and massive inner bank with timber-lined gateway. With its outworks, the complex at Hambledon apparently extended to over 28 ha.

In the 1920s, it was proposed that a Marconi wireless station should be set up on Windmill Hill, the classic causewayed camp. Alexander Keiller (of the Keiller jam and marmalade family) excavated there. He is remarkable for having bought Avebury henge and part of the Kennet Avenue, where he subsequently carried out excavations. He was an admirer of Pitt-Rivers, and his excavations at Windmill Hill revived the General's methods with some success. Inside the camp he uncovered a rectangular enclosure defined by a trench which had presumably taken a palisade. It contained nothing but pits. This showed features in common with the 'long mortuary enclosure' at Fussell's Lodge (see p. 126) which was used for the exposing of corpses, and it may be that this is further evidence for this possible function of causewayed camps.

Henges and henge-builders

Every day, cars stream across the faint traces of one of pre-historic man's most monumental achievements in Britain – Durrington Walls. Lying some 4.8km north of Stonehenge on Salisbury Plain, it is now practically obliterated, but thanks to the excavations carried out there in the 1960s it is possible to recreate this remarkable sanctuary in the mind's eye.

To the pious pilgrim approaching Durrington across the broad sweep of Salisbury Plain, the first impression must have been that of the gleaming chalk of the ditch and its quarry bank, a white weal in the verdant green of the countryside, for by the time Durrington was built this part of Wessex was already cleared of dense woodland. Approaching the sacred circle by way of one of the two opposed entrances, a proper sense of one's own insignificance would have been gained by a glance into the ditch on either side of the causeway – an impressive 5.64m deep in parts, and up to 12.8m wide, its chalky bottom flat and bare, except where

46 Durrington Walls, Wiltshire, during excavation, 1967. This is the largest of a series of late Neolithic henge monuments, which are defined by a ditch and external bank. Excavation revealed circular timber buildings within it. The ditch was up to 5.64m deep and 12.8m wide. Such 'henges' were ritual sites of the later Neolithic, which seem to have succeeded causewayed camps. The photograph shows the huge post-holes of one of the circular buildings

tufts of grass and weeds had started to take hold again in the first steps towards carpeting the whole once more with grass. The chalk quarried from the ditch was piled up outside it, and who can tell what awesome sight might have greeted the visitor at the entrace – skulls on stakes, perhaps? Carved wooden effigies, painted like totem poles? Timber tables, on which the dead decomposed, the smell of death mingling with the wafting smoke from the two huge timber buildings set inside the henge proper?

The interior of the monument covered over 10 hectares. Even before the ditch was dug out, a circular timber building had been erected on the site, and this was replaced at the time the henge was constructed with a larger, more imposing edifice. Now there were two, each with its sloping roof of thatch. The southern building measured 36m across, its roof supported by six concentric circles of posts. The northern was similar, but may have had a central lantern to let smoke out and light in.

What was the function of these timber pavilions? One at least had seen habitation, for domestic refuse lay around, and there was a central hearth to warm its occupants and perhaps to cook some food. Outside, a chalk platform may also have served as a cooking place. They may have been the communal huts of the tribal elders or officiating priests, or they could quite simply have been meeting-places, where men gathered round the camp-fire to 'smoke the pipe of peace' and discuss territorial boundaries, stock, or how much corn they wanted for their prize heifers. Outside, in the open spaces, there may well have been the hubbub and jostle of an oriental market place, as axe-traders spread out their wares and itinerant cobblers fashioned shoes while their customers waited or where the pot vendors offered 'two pots for the price of one, for one day only'.

Durrington Walls is one of a series of late Neolithic and early Bronze Age ritual monuments known as 'henges'. The earliest date from around 3500–3300 BC, and they thus overlap with causewayed camps which had been under construction since 4000 BC or even slightly earlier. Causewayed camps and henges are clearly related, and they obviously served a similar function, but it seems unlikely that henges evolved out of causewayed camps, since the earliest henges are found in the north-west, outside causewayed camp country.

The most elaborate, later, henges are concentrated in Wessex, and may owe something to Irish influence in their design. Henges take their name from Stonehenge (the word literally means 'hanging' and refers to the Stonehenge trilithons), which in its first phase had no standing stones at all but instead a circular ditch broken by a single entrance causeway and a bank of earth quarried from the ditch. Such henges, with single entrance and ditch, are typical of the late Neolithic, and were probably put up by the users of Grooved ware. More elaborate henges were built later, with double entrances.

Like causewayed camps before them, henges are frequently associated with stone axes, and one of their func-

47 Restored late Neolithic Grooved ware pot from Durrington Walls, Wiltshire, along with a 'ritual' chalk axe and a bone pin. Axes are frequently associated with henge monuments, and may have had a symbolic function

tions may have been the marketing of them. At Llandegai, one of the earliest henges known, a mint axe from Great Langdale was buried under the bank, and there are 'ritual' chalk axes from Woodhenge (see below, p. 117). Although originating in the west, most henges are found in the east of Britain. This is partly to be explained by geographical features – it was easier to dig the ditches in the east. In the west too, stone circles were developed, and by the Beaker period, henges and stone circles are frequently found amalgamated (see p. 160). Although stone circles were not put up by the users of Grooved ware, wooden circles which may have been their prototypes were.

Timber structures inside henges were not peculiar to Durrington Walls. They are found in a group of giant henges in Wessex, all of which are in excess of 250m in diameter, notably Marden and Mount Pleasant, and they have been found standing on their own. The most famous of the timber 'meeting-houses' is the structure known as Woodhenge, which stands only a few yards from Durrington Walls. Revealed by aerial photography in 1925, and excavated in 1926–8, it consisted of a ditched enclosure with a single entrance entirely filled with a building defined by six circles of posts. Just off-centre was a grave containing an infant, its skull cleft in two, only one of several possible instances of infant sacrifice in early prehistoric Britain (see p. 154 for others). On Overton Hill, not far from Avebury, concrete pegs now mark the post-holes of a structure with a complex history. It began with the building of a small hut, a mere 4.1m in diameter, which was elaborated and rebuilt at least once, its roof supported by the now-familiar concentric rings of posts. This was replaced by a circle of timber posts, which in turn gave way to a stone circle. Nothing of it now remains, as it was smashed up in the early eighteenth century. In 1724 Stukeley recorded that a farmer, Griffin by name, was responsible for the vandalism, and thereby 'gained a little dirty profit'.

Moonshine and Stonehenge

The mathematical and astronomical abilities of the Neolithic people are hotly debated. During the Neolithic, and in the succeeding early Bronze Age, there is evidence for growing sophistication in the planning of ritual sites. It would be wrong to infer from the evidence of archaeology that pre-historic man in Britain had an interest in science and

48 Woodhenge, Wiltshire, a late Neolithic ritual site adjacent to Durrington Walls. The concrete pegs mark the position of post-holes first discovered by aerial photography in 1925. An infant burial with its skull cleft in two was found just off-centre. It was probably a building not unlike those found inside Durrington Walls

49 Arbor Low, Derbyshire, from the air. This is a classic henge monument, with its ditch inside its bank and pair of opposed entrances. It was later elaborated with the construction of a circle of standing stones within it, which had in its centre a 'cove' (two of the stones of this are visible in the photo) associated with a burial to its east. The pock-marked mound at the rear of the henge is a Bronze Age round barrow, its top cratered by antiquaries' excavations

knowledge for its own sake, and that his concern with the heavens was either scientific or metaphysical. Almost certainly, religious interest in astronomy was connected with practical considerations – both were significant in so far as both might control the smooth running of the farming calendar. Not that farmers often need a calendar to tell them when to plant or when to harvest – the pattern of the seasons makes it fairly clear. But it is better to make doubly sure.

Although families might be scattered, it is quite clear that society in general was well organized, for organization is imperative for the specialization of labour that makes axe-factories viable propositions, and which can ensure the even distribution of manufactured products over a wide area. Organization too was necessary for the marketing of pottery, for the importing from abroad of jade axes (even if these were brought in by itinerant pedlars), for the construction of trackways such as those in the Somerset Levels and for the erection of earthworks such as the henges and many types of tombs. Estimates of manpower required for this or that prehistoric project are popular diversions amongst scholars, but can only be a rough guide since prehistoric man was in the habit of using shoulder-blade shovels, antler picks and baskets, unlike his modern counterparts on building sites.

The mathematical precision displayed in the original laying out of monuments and in astronomical calculation and observation seems to have coincided with the henge-building phase of the late Neolithic, and the widespread use of Grooved ware. Some interest in mathematical precision, however, is apparent in the Overton Sanctuary which in its earlier phases dated to around 3400 BC. In each successive phase the number of posts used in the construction was doubled or the diameter of the building was doubled without structural reason. Some megalithic chambered tombs also show a concern with mathematical proportions (p. 130).

It is in the first phase of the Stonehenge monument that both mathematical precision and a concern for the heavens can be most readily observed. The phase of this henge (Stonehenge I) has been dated to around 2700 BC and the builders were, like those at Durrington, the users of Grooved ware. Stonehenge I called for at least 30,000 man-hours of labour to construct. Whatever purpose other henges may have served, this most famous example was certainly designed partly for the observation of midsummer and midwinter. Outside the earthwork enclosure stood the Heel Stone, which may even have been erected before the henge was built. Two massive stones may have flanked the single entrance to the enclosure. Fifty-three stake-holes have been found in eleven incomplete rows, six deep, across the entrance. They are oriented on the extreme midwinter risings of the moon from its maximum to the point at which it intersects with midsummer sunrise; nine years would have separated these events. The number of posts suggests that observations were made over a period of a century or more, and would have been used to fix the times of midsummer and midwinter celebrations. These stake-holes predate the construction of the henge, indicating that observations were being made even before the first enclosure existed, perhaps soon after 3000 BC. When the henge was constructed the stakes were replaced by a single line of more massive posts to the north-east, near the Heel Stone, as the original markers would have blocked the entrance. Three posts outside the henge served to align midsummer sunset and midwinter moonset.

The overall siting of Stonehenge I is also significant. At this point the extreme north and south risings and settings of sun and moon were at right-angles to one another, whereas a few miles away the cross-alignments would have lain on the sides of a skewed parallelogram.

The Aubrey Holes were dug around the interior perimeter of the henge in its earliest period, if not before the henge itself was constructed. They may not have been excavated at one time, but they were probably marked and on occasion may have been reopened, to judge from the fact that cremation burials were apparently inserted in some of them. It is possible to place a right-angled triangle over holes 7, 28 and 56, which can be matched exactly in each corresponding set of three. The sides of the triangle are in accordance with the 'Megalithic Yard' (0.829m), the standard unit of reckoning in the British Neolithic and Bronze Age.

Tombs – the beginnings of architecture

Can there be any monuments in the world that have attracted so much bizarre theorizing or which have played such a prominent role in folklore as the megalithic monuments of western Europe? Megaliths are still being built. Leaving aside a series of eighteenth-century follies, all over Wales, for instance, can be seen the stone Gorsedd circles, which were recently set up for the purpose of celebrating the Eisteddfod. At Maryhill, Washington, DC, there is a First World War memorial in the form of a reconstruction of Stonehenge. In 1958 a megalithic setting inscribed with alchemist's symbols was set up on the front of Cambridge University's Chemical Laboratories. In Belgium a fake chambered tomb's chamber was erected to commemorate the first use of gas by the Germans against the French and Belgians in 1915. Old chambered tombs have been put to a diversity of uses – as bakehouses, barns, stores for farm implements, a café and even a garage. Witches still favour megaliths as suitable places to hold covens, and some people have been buried under re-erected standing stones or, in the case of a lady at Confolens, Charente, in France, in a carved sarcophagus set on the capstone of a re-erected tomb. Most of the theories concerning stone monuments relate to those of the Bronze Age, but here we must consider only those put up by Neolithic Man – chambered tombs.

Long before the pharaohs were instructing sweaty slaves to construct the pyramids, the early farmers of north-west Europe could call upon the services of individuals who were highly skilled architects. The edifices they put up, the Neolithic chambered tombs, are amongst the finest achievements of early prehistoric man. They appear all the more remarkable to modern minds, since they pre-date any comparable sepulchres of the civilized eastern Mediterranean. The realization that the tombs can be dated in some areas as far back as 4800 BC has been one of the most important recent advances in knowledge. However, none in Britain is older than about 4000 BC.

The most casual observer can easily learn to distinguish chambered tombs from other ancient monuments, since all have features in common. With the exception of a few which are rock-cut, they are built with massive undressed boulders (hence 'megalithic' or 'big stone'), sometimes combined with dry-stone walling. All were intended for multiple burials, which were incorporated into a mound of earth or stone. There are two main types, *passage graves*, in which a tunnel leads to one or more chambers within the mound, and *gallery graves* in which the burials are laid within a gallery. Related are simple structures often called *dolmens* or *cromlechs*. These consist of a chamber composed of a capstone which characteristically rests on three uprights.

The earliest known megalithic tombs are found in Brittany, with other, independently evolved, examples in Scandinavia and Iberia. Megalithic tombs of different types have been discovered in places as far from one another as Polynesia and Japan, Abyssinia and the Caucasus. Nineteenth-century antiquaries considered that all megalithic chambered tombs belonged to a single period of time and were representative of a stage in the evolution of architecture. In 1872 in his classic study *Rude Stone Monuments in All Countries* James Fergusson voiced the view that 'the style of architecture to which these monuments belong is a style like Gothic, Grecian, Egyptian, Buddhist or any other', and that all were erected 'by partially civilized races after they had come into contact with the Romans, and most of them may be considered as belonging to the first ten centuries of the Christian era'.

Although Fergusson's dating was not universally accepted, many antiquaries favoured his view that megaliths were an architectural fashion spread among many different peoples. To Elliot Smith and Perry they were an architectural fashion spread from ancient Egypt – where else? To many other writers in the earlier part of this century they were certainly the outcome of diffusion from some centre in a migration or series of migrations.

Gordon Childe adhered to his view of modified diffusionism (see p. 20) when writing about megaliths. To Childe, the chambered tombs were the work of 'megalithic missionaries' who spread their ideas about tomb-building along with the faith that gave rise to them at some stage during the Neolithic. Childe believed that the homeland of chambered tombs was to be found in the Mediterranean. 'Missionaries', he wrote in 1940, 'from various centres in Atlantic Europe brought several versions of the megalithic religion to the British Isles.' He went on to observe:

On a quest for the Isles of the Blest or Givers of Life fanatics might brave the perils of a voyage across the Bay of Biscay to the Bristol Channel or the Firth of Clyde. Once wafted to the shores of the British Isles, such adventurers might be accepted as wizards by the local Windmill Hill peasants, and installed as chiefs.
(*Prehistoric Communities of the British Isles*)

This enchanting picture endured until the advent of radio-carbon dating, when gradually prehistorians began to realize that the idea of dissemination from a Mediterranean source would not do. The tombs of north-west Europe were for one thing appreciably older than any possible 'ante-cedents' in the Mediterranean. Furthermore, the pattern of regional development did not fit in with a theory of universal tomb development. It became clear that tombs developed independently in different regions, and pre-historians were forced to look again at the evidence for how megalithic chambered tombs came to develop into the characteristic structures to be seen in the British landscape.

It is now apparent that Neolithic people constructed diverse edifices for the collective disposal of their dead. The earliest were what have been termed *mortuary enclosures*. These were roughly rectangular or trapezoidal and were surrounded by a ditch – often they had an internal quarry bank and a palisade. Entry was through a timber portal. These mortuary enclosures were intended for the exposure of corpses which were laid out to rot either in timber *mortuary houses* inside the enclosure, or perhaps on the roof of the portals where they would be safe from marauding animals. Mortuary enclosures were no doubt the setting for a variety of rituals, the nature of which we can only guess.

At some stage the idea of burying the mortuary enclosure and associated structures under an earthen mound, was introduced, probably from the Continent. The resultant mounds, which are trapezoidal and usually higher at one end than the other, are termed *earthen long barrows*; in earlier literature they are often misleadingly termed 'unchambered long barrows'.

Before very long some communities began constructing stone versions of the timber portals of the mortuary enclosures. These consisted of a massive slab (the roof on which the bodies were laid), supported by two or three uprights. Prehistorians term them *proto-megaliths*, and the cromlechs of north Wales are typical examples. Just as the timber portals had been incorporated into the mounds of long barrows, so were proto-megaliths incorporated into the mounds of earth or stone that were constructed at this time. The proto-megalith might be found at one end of a mound, where it formed a 'false portal'. This happened in the Cotswolds, where there are a series of tombs with burials in the sides of the mound and a false portal at the end. A classic example is Belas Knap in Gloucestershire, where the 'false portal' is set within an ornate concave façade. Elsewhere they may have been completely covered by the mound, which might also cover later, more elaborate types of megalithic structure. This happened at Dyffryn Ardudwy in Gwynedd.

Proto-megaliths are found in Cornwall, Wales, Ireland and in a variant form in western Scotland. Here, round the mouth of the Clyde, can be traced the evolution of *gallery graves* out of simple box-like structures. Soon after 4000 BC the box-like cells were fronted in this area by a second, third and even fourth chamber, a pair of portal stones being added as an entrance.

Other types of gallery grave were being developed around the same time in the Severn-Cotswold region. A classic example is West Kennet, near Avebury, in Wiltshire. Such gallery graves as this were furnished with an elaborate façade, and profoundly influenced the development of the Clyde tombs, the new ideas perhaps being transmitted by way of the Irish Sea. The outcome were the Clyde Cairns, as they are called, of which Monamore on Arran is a classic example.

50 Dyffryn Ardudwy, Gwynedd, a classic example of a multi-period chambered tomb. The western chamber (*left*) was built first, and is a classic example of a portal dolmen which was contained in its own cairn. The second chamber was built subsequently to a different design, then both were incorporated into a single large mound of stones. This excavation showed how chambered tombs could be built in several stages

123

51   The portal stones of Cashtal yn Ard, which faced the semi-circular courtyard of a megalithic chambered tomb in the Isle of Man. The cairn covering the tomb has long since been robbed, but the forecourt is still impressive

Around 3500 BC or slightly earlier an era of religious zeal was heralded by the arrival, fully fledged, of a new type of chambered tomb from the Continent. This was the passage grave. They probably caught on in Britain because already some passage graves were being developed out of earlier gallery graves. There are two groups of 'native' passage graves, one found in south-west Scotland known as the Bargrennan group after a site in Kirkcudbright, the other in the Cotswolds, where the passages set into the long sides of tombs like Belas Knap represent a development from simple box-like chambers.

The classic examples of the exotic passage graves are to be found in Ireland, and are known as the Boyne tombs as they are concentrated in the Boyne valley. The most famous are Newgrange, Knowth and Dowth. They are very sophisticated structures, and display a distinctive art, known as 'Passage grave art'. They influenced the development of tombs in northern Scotland, notably the Maes Howe group in Orkney, and there is an outlier in north Wales, at Barclodiad-y-Gawres.

A series of sites can be used to chronicle the early development of mortuary enclosures and earthen long barrows. At Normanton Down (Wiltshire) a long mortuary enclosure was excavated without any covering mound, its ditch dug in irregular sections like a causewayed camp, a timber porch at its east end. No funerary remains were found in it – either the bodies had been taken away after rotting or it never saw

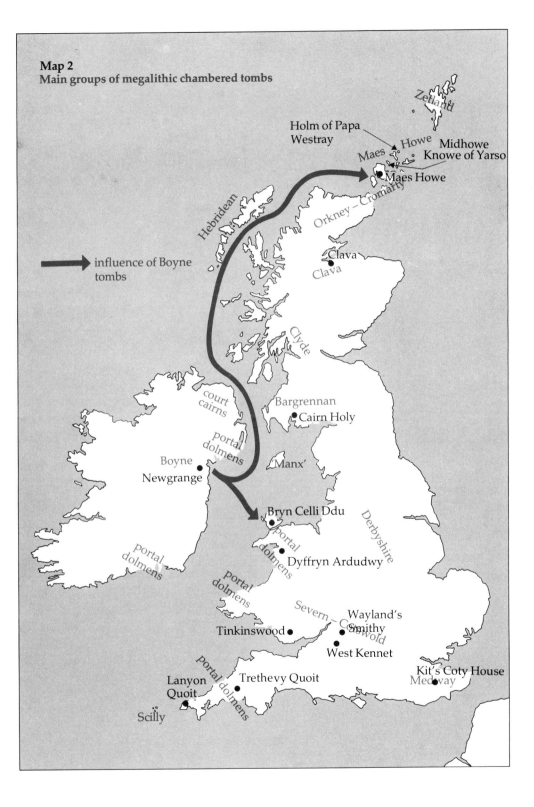

Map 2
Main groups of megalithic chambered tombs

Holm of Papa
Westray

Maes Howe

Midhowe
Knowe of Yarso

Maes Howe

Orkney – Cromarty

Hebridean

→ influence of Boyne
  tombs

Clava
Clava

Clyde

court
cairns

Bargrennan
Cairn Holy

portal
dolmens

Boyne
Newgrange

Manx'

Bryn Celli Ddu

portal
dolmens

Derbyshire

portal
dolmens

Dyffryn Ardudwy

portal
dolmens

Severn – Cotswold

Wayland's
Smithy

Tinkinswood

West Kennet

Kit's Coty House
Medway

portal dolmens

Lanyon
Quoit

Trethevy Quoit

Scilly

use. The classic examples of mortuary enclosures, mortuary houses and porches underlie long barrows. The earliest of these to be dated by radio-carbon is Lambourn (Berkshire), assigned to around 4340 BC. Fussell's Lodge (Wiltshire), Seamer Moor (Yorkshire) and Dalladies (Kincardine) show that long barrows were widespread in the period 4200–3800 BC.

A classic long barrow is that of Nutbane (Hampshire). The farmers here had constructed a timber building, measuring 4.9m by 4.3m, within a banked burial enclosure. The site saw long use before the barrow was put up. The first 'mortuary house' was replaced by a larger example (12.2m by 6.1m), which was further elaborated by flanking façades. The original banked enclosure was replaced by fencing, and when the last burials had been laid to rest the entrance through the fence was blocked and the enclosure filled with earth. The forecourt was ritually fired, and a huge mound, 51.8m long and 21.3m broad, was heaped up over the whole, leaving us only to imagine the details of the dramatic rituals that must have been enacted several thousand years ago.

In some cases the enclosures were furnished with elaborate entrances, for example at Wor Barrow (excavated by Pitt-Rivers), Fussell's Lodge or Wayland's Smithy (Berkshire).

Both Fussell's Lodge and Wayland's Smithy had mortu-

52 A long barrow sits amid a cemetery of later Bronze Age round barrows at Lambourn, Berkshire. The site is known as Seven Barrows, though there are in fact more, a frequent occurrence with sites of this name! Earthen long barrows were the forerunners of megalithic chambered tombs, and overlap chronologically with them

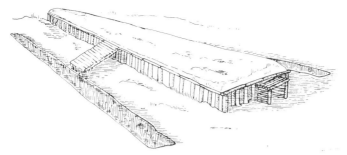

Figure 1   Reconstruction of Fussell's Lodge long barrow

ary houses of 'ridge-tent' form, with a ridge-pole supported by two end posts. The story unfolded at Wayland's Smithy is fascinating, for on this site not only the building of a mortuary house can be traced, but also the subsequent erection of a megalithic chambered tomb.

Wayland's Smithy stands in a leafy setting in the heart of southern England, near the venerable prehistoric track-way known as the Ridgeway, and less than a mile from two of the most famous Iron Age monuments in Britain, the chalk-cut Uffington White Horse, and Uffington Castle hill-fort. Wayland's Smithy is a part of England's heritage inextricably woven into the fabric of folklore. Wayland was a Scandinavian god, who, according to tradition, was forced to shoe horses for a living after the coming of Christianity. He was never seen – if a wayfarer required his mount to be

53 West Kennet long barrow, near Avebury, Wilts. The long trapezoidal mound covers at its broadest end a megalithic chambered tomb of Severn-Cotswold type. From an imposing façade flanked by megalithic uprights, a passage leads to chambers lit by sky-lights. It is a gallery grave – lateral chambers open from the main passage

shod, he had to leave a groat on the capstone of the tomb and go away. During his absence the animal would be shod. Wayland's great achievement was the shoeing of the White Horse itself. It was also said that if iron were left at the Smithy it would be turned into horseshoes – when the site was first excavated in the nineteenth century some iron bars were found, but no finished horseshoes.

The first funeral monument at Wayland's Smithy was the timber 'ridge tent' mortuary house, its roof supported by two massive half tree trunks. This was found to have contained about fourteen individuals – the insect remains showed clearly that the corpses had been left to decompose for some time in the open air. Over this structure the mourners had heaped a low oval mound – they had dug two flanking quarry ditches for the purpose.

Later, this earthen long barrow was defaced when a chambered tomb of Severn-Cotswold type was built. With its ornate façade of upright stones, this had contained the remains of at least eight people.

The transition from timber to stone can be illustrated from Lochhill in Dumfriesshire. The first phase of construction here was a rectangular timber building with straight timber

54 View into the interior of West Kennet long barrow. The bodies in the lateral chambers had been left to decay prior to burial, and their bones had been stacked in rows

façade which had been burnt down and then covered by a long cairn of stones containing a chamber without burials, and with a fine stone façade which replaced its timber predecessor. It dated from soon after 4000 BC.

Recent studies have demonstrated that the mounds covering chambered tombs may hide several separate structures; in other words, the construction of a cairn or mound of stones was simply the last operation in a series of ritual observances.

This can be readily demonstrated at Dyffryn Ardudwy in Gwynedd, where the first structure was a 'proto-megalith' with a characteristic pair of flanking portal stones – a type known as a 'portal dolmen'. This the Neolithic worshippers had incorporated in a cairn of stones since there was no adequate soil. In front of it was a pit containing early pottery. Later generations had built a rectangular megalithic chamber to its east. A huge rectangular cairn then enveloped it and the first tomb, and was furnished with a forecourt, which had been ritually blocked with great elaboration.

129

The triumph of tomb-building

The Boyne valley passage graves of Ireland are among the finest in Europe. Although they may have developed from local types, they owed much to influence from Iberia. Newgrange and other examples are contemporary, for instance, with the passage graves of the Almerian culture, and in their concern with the position of the sun and in their mathematical precision they herald developments in Neolithic Britain. Contacts between the two areas seem to be proven by distinctively Iberian objects found on Irish sites, such as decorated stone basins and particular types of bone pin. At Newgrange, the finest of the Irish sites, recent excavations have shown that the builders were concerned with solar observation. Above the entrance to the tomb a roof box was hidden by a decorated, removable false lintel. The box was constructed to allow light to shine into the passage after the entrance had been blocked. Experiment and measurement showed that a few minutes after dawn on midwinter's day the sun's rays steal down the passage, filter across the main chamber and finally illuminate the side chamber at the rear. The opening of the roof box was blocked at other times by an imported slab of quartz.

The architects of the Boyne tombs had an influence on tomb builders in northern Scotland. Here visitors can see the Maes Howe tombs, whose builders were almost cer-

56 Passage grave art at its best can be observed in the tombs of the Boyne Valley in Ireland, particularly at Knowth, Dowth and Newgrange. This elaborately ornamented stone came to light during excavations at Newgrange by Professor M. J. O'Kelly. Known as kerbstone 52, it is diametrically opposite the entrance stone

tainly the users of Grooved ware pottery. The type-site is Maes Howe itself. This outstanding feat of Neolithic architecture has with reason been claimed to be the finest example of prehistoric architecture north of the Alps. Because of the way in which the Orcadian sandstone splits along the bedding plane into neat slabs, Maes Howe is superbly constructed with a corbelled vault which rose to a height of about 4.6m above the floor – off this small burial chambers opened. The slabs (some of which weighed up to 3

tons) were carefully levelled and plumbed, small slivers of stone being used to underpin those that were not lying true. Maes Howe is 35m in diameter.

A somewhat smaller example is Quanterness (24m), where six side burial chambers open from the corbelled chamber. Quanterness had not been totally pillaged in the past. It was re-opened in 1972 by a team from Southampton University, who came upon vast numbers of bone fragments – 12,500 of humans – which represented perhaps 157 individuals. Since archaeologists examined only the deposits on the floor of the main chamber and one at the side, it was estimated that up to 400 people had been interred in the tomb. Pieces of Grooved ware pots lay on the floor, and there were signs of ritual burning. The human bodies had decomposed elsewhere. Quanterness was dated to around 3000 BC – it remained in use until 2450 BC or thereabouts.

57 These remarkable chalk drums are decorated with patterns similar to those of the passage graves and of Grooved ware pottery. They also bear stylized faces with pronounced eyebrows, and similar faces appear on occasion in chambered tombs. Although stylistically late Neolithic, they were found with a Copper Age beaker in a barrow at Folkton, Yorkshire. The shape of the drums recalls that of some Iberian pots, and the type of eyes can also be found in the same area. Diameter of largest drum: 14.3cm

131

58 Wideford Hill, Orkney, one of the 'Maes Howe' family of chambered tombs. Note the concentric walling, designed to retain the cairn and not originally intended to be seen. Due to the nature of Orkney flagstone, the Maes Howe tombs show astonishing sophistication in their construction

Ritual and belief in Neolithic burial practices

What do the megalithic chambered tombs and earthen long barrows mean in human terms? It is very difficult to be certain. Studies of the distribution of chambered tombs in Orkney on the island of Rousay suggested that these were the work of tribal groups of fairly equal status. Each tomb commanded a unit of arable land capable of supporting between 25 and 50 people – this estimate was achieved by assuming that 0.4 ha of land was necessary to feed one person. If allowances are made for the need to leave land to lie fallow, this indicates that between 0.8 and 8.1 hectares should be allowed per head of the population. The calculations for Rousay indicate that the island had a Neolithic population of between 300 and 650 people, in 13 territories, each with its own tomb.

Twenty-five to fifty people could not have built a chambered tomb on their own unless over an immensely long period of time. The megalithic chambered tombs were clearly the result of collaboration between the tribes or families in neighbouring territories. It is likely that they were more than just tombs – they were 'shrines' and the tribal foci of each group. On comparison with modern tribal groups, the building of a tomb may have been an occasion when there was a lavish feast laid on by the group that wanted the

(a)

(b)

59 (a) Maes Howe, Orkney, perhaps the finest chambered tomb in north-west Europe. The mound rises to a height of 7.32m

59 (b) The interior of Maes Howe, looking out down the entrance passage, which is 11m long. The central chamber is 4.6m square, with burial chambers opening out from it. So neat is the masonry, it is impossible to pass a knife blade between the stones in many cases. The tomb was broken into by Norse Crusaders who carved runic inscriptions on the walls – some of these can be seen on the edge of the tall upright stone to the right of the entrance, and the wall at the far right of the picture. They recorded carrying off treasure from the howe (mound) but this is unlikely

sepulchre erected, to which neighbouring tribes were invited. In return for the comestibles and entertainment, the incomers assisted in the erection of the monument. The possession of a fine tomb would bestow prestige on its owners. It is notable that evidence for ritual meals and the deliberate breaking of pots has been found in the excavations of several megalithic tombs.

133

60 The exterior of an unconsolidated Maes Howe type of tomb, Knowe of Lairo, Rousay, Orkney

What kind of ritual was involved at burials? There are signs that skulls and long bones were often carefully separated, and skulls were frequently set upright. Various offerings were made – of pots and flint implements, for instance. Ceramic vessels are always found shattered, and are usually incomplete, suggesting that they may have been destroyed in order to release the 'spirit'; sherds may have been removed for ritual reasons. Small bones may have been conveyed elsewhere for similar purposes – this would explain the instances of incomplete skeletons. Now and again the pottery was laid in a heap, apart from the burials, sometimes in hollows in the floor.

Fires were sometimes lit in the chambers – some of these were relatively small, others were conflagrations that burned the bodies. Offerings of food are indicated by the presence of animal bones. Several Orcadian tombs have yielded dog bones which may have been offerings made in connection with hunting ceremonies. Now and again a final burial was made after the blocking of the passage – perhaps these were the 'guardians' of the tombs.

There are a few hints of rituals of a more bizarre nature. At Maiden Castle, Dorset, an elongated bank barrow over a third of a mile in length produced the mutilated body of a young man. He had been beheaded, the skull shattered and the limbs amputated. There is reason for thinking that these are remnants of a cannibal feast, though of course a particularly savage killing could also explain the condition of the corpse.

Silbury Hill

Of the many late Neolithic ritual sites, one poses a particular puzzle. This is the great mound of Silbury Hill. Described as the largest man-made mound in Europe, it would have taken a gang of 500 men fifteen years to pile it up, if they worked continuously. Clearly it was not the enterprise of a small community working in a piecemeal fashion, but the communal effort of people scattered through a wide tract of countryside. Silbury was commenced somewhere between 2900 and 2500BC. It covers 5½ acres (2.2 hectares), and rises 130ft (40m) above the surrounding countryside. Various attempts have been made to unlock the riddle of why it was erected – a shaft was driven through it in 1849, and in 1969–70 amid great publicity the BBC sponsored a further excavation in which the centre of the mound was pen-

61 Silbury Hill, the largest man-made mound in Europe. Of Neolithic date, it stands near Avebury in Wiltshire. Several excavations have attempted to determine its purpose, without any real success. It covers 2.1 ha and rises 40m above the surrounding countryside

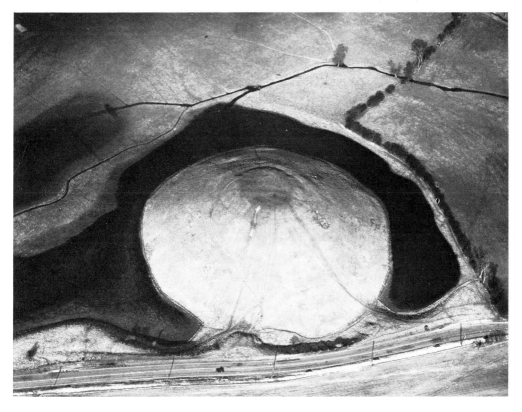

etrated. In the heart of Silbury the excavators found no gold, no burial, no ancient treasures, merely a series of randomly placed boulders.

The mound itself was constructed in three phases, beginning with a conical mound 5.5m high, which was capped with another of chalk rubble, which in turn was built up with more chalk from the 7m-deep quarry ditch. Silbury cannot be proved to be sepulchral (though of course it is so large that it cannot be excavated totally, so it is possible that a burial has been missed). The most likely solution to its function seems to be that it was connected with astronomical observation, though this too cannot be indisputably proved and many other theories have been woven around it. Vast and mysterious, it epitomizes the fascination of Neolithic Britain.

The thinkers – the first steps to civilization (Copper and Bronze Ages)

Chapter four

Unique in the collection of finds from prehistoric Britain is a strange bowl that was found in a bog near Caergwrle Castle, Clwyd, in 1823. It is oval, carved out of a block of oak, with a rounded bottom, and is inlaid with gold leaf on which linear patterns have been finely incised. A series of over twenty discs ornamented with concentric circles adorns the rim. Below this gold plates have been inlaid into triangular cuts, the plates engraved with vertical lines. Three zig-zag lines are deeply cut below this, and along the bottom lies a row of transverse triangular cuts. At one end there is a pair of 'eyes' – there were probably a similar pair, now lost, at the other. In many ways the Caergwrle bowl epitomizes the problems of interpretations posed by the material remains of the Bronze Age.

Most experts agree that it probably represents a ship. The zig-zag lines are taken to be waves, the rows of concentric circles are seen to be warriors' shields hanging over the bows. The triangular inlays are the oars, and the 'eyes' are those carved on the prow to ward off evil. But is this interpretation correct? Did Bronze Age warriors really put to sea like Vikings, with their shields hung over the sides of the ship, and did they really adorn the prows with eyes like those that could be seen on the 'beaks' of classical warships? Were Bronze Age warriors really similar to their counterparts in Homeric Greece – seafaring heroes?

And is the Caergwrle bowl really Bronze Age in date? The other possibility is that it belongs to the Iron Age. The only other ship model from this part of the world is the gold Iron Age ship from Broighter, Ireland. The Caergwrle example is quite unlike it, and very different from the boats with high prows that are depicted on Iron Age coins. On the other hand, the type of ornament on the Caergwrle bowl is characteristic of the early Bronze Age 'sun discs' and very reminiscent of the engravings found on Bronze Age lunulae (gold collars) and gorgets produced in Ireland. Indeed, late Bronze Age Irish gold-work boasts identical concentric ring patterns similarly engraved – they appear, for example, on a superb gorget from Gleninsheen, Co. Clare, and on a dress-fastener of the same period from Clones, Co. Monaghan. In all probability, therefore, the Caergwrle bowl was made in the late Bronze Age, perhaps in the eighth century BC, and possibly it was imported from Ireland or made under Irish influence. It is true that round Bronze Age shields with concentric ornament have been found in late Bronze Age Britain, but the roundels on the bowl could represent the sun with as much probability. Could this 'ship' be the product of a Bronze Age sun cult?

There is, too, the question of why such a ship model was made. It could be a ship of the dead intended to take souls to the afterlife – the objection to this is that ship burials are unknown in the Bronze Age or Iron Age in Britain. Puzzle piles on puzzle as the experts make informed guesses about the model, but it is impossible to be sure of any of the apparent inferences.

One aspect is certainly true. If the Caergwrle bowl does represent a ship, it is perfectly compatible with the fine craft that are known to have glided over Bronze Age waters. A very elaborate plank-built boat was found at North Ferriby (Yorkshire) and dated to the late Bronze Age. Originally it would have been about 15.2m long with a maximum beam of about 2.4m, with cross-struts and seats for oarsmen. All the timbers were carefully jointed and sewn together with yew withies before the whole vessel was caulked. In the summer of 1979 divers were investigating the wreck of a late Bronze Age vessel that went down off the south coast of England with its cargo of bronze-work. It had clearly been a trading vessel operating between England and France.

The Caergwrle bowl in many ways symbolizes the essential elements of Bronze Age Britain. The period was that of a heroic society, thirsty for gold and eager for power. It was a society in which men worked together to achieve their aims, of which some of the most ambitious seem to have been the erection of complex ritual monuments that are amongst the most famous landmarks in Britain. It was an adventurous

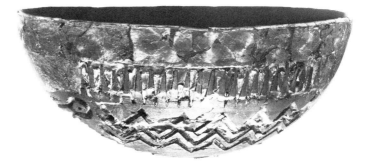

62 The Caergwrle bowl, Clwyd. Found in a bog near Caergwrle Castle in 1823, it is believed to represent a boat. It is made of wood, inlaid with gold leaf. The circles round the rim have been taken to represent shields, the triangles beneath oars, and the chevron pattern at the bottom waves. Late Bronze Age. Length: 21 cm

society with ever-expanding frontiers of awareness, ready to trade far and wide for the goods it required. Boats may well have been integral to its system of communications, for much of Britain was still wild and difficult to traverse except by waterways. The people were warriors as well as farmers, craftsmen as well as labourers. In Bronze Age society can be seen the seeds of the culture that was to flower under the stimulus of the Celts from Continental Europe; the insular culture of Iron Age Britain. The Caergwrle bowl was probably an offering to a lake god, and it is notable that such gifts were common in Celtic society centuries later. The bowl bridges the two ages of higher barbarism of prehistoric Europe – the Bronze Age and the Iron Age.

The sources (the Copper Age)

There is no real divide between the late Neolithic and the early metal ages in Britain. The advent of copper technology brought about few immediate changes in society. Some incomers and innovators worked metal, others still followed their ancestral traditions and used stone. Little by little a few other changes made more impact on life until effortlessly people had slipped through what has become known as the Copper Age into the Bronze Age. The introduction of the wheel was to the Bronze Age people perhaps the most far-reaching change, though from the point of view of archaeologists, differences in funeral rites and ceramic styles assume vital importance in chronicling the period.

The metal ages are made more definite in character by the jargon inherited from Victorian fantasies. Nondescript pots, for instance, were honoured with such romantic names as 'incense cups', 'food vessels' or 'grape cups'. Possibly the ultimate in obscurantism was achieved by Canon Greenwell, who bequeathed to prehistory the 'carp's tongue' sword. Greenwell was a fanatical fisherman who invented the fly known as Greenwell's Glory, and as no prehistorian seems to have had a more intimate knowledge of the anatomy of the carp that he, the appellation of the sword has endured. The antiquaries also caused endless confusion by calling axes 'celts', and by using the word 'palstave' to describe a stage in the development of the Bronze Age axe.

The age of metal may be said to begin with the arrival of the copper-using Beaker people from the Continent in the late Neolithic period. There were several groups, of whom the earliest arrived around 3000 BC. Metal made its appearance around 2500 BC, gold being used almost as early as copper. Although material distinctive of the Beaker people has been found in chambered tombs the newcomers introduced single burials under an earthen mound or barrow. The Beaker people (as well as those of the early Bronze Age) also used new types of henges and stone circles.

The first man to use copper in Britain was indeed a pioneer. The metal brought the obvious benefits of providing better edge tools, and also led to new and specialized knowledge. Any farmer with some practice could probably have produced a stone tool, but without the technical know-how no man of the fields would have been able to make an adequate copper axe. The need for specialized knowledge must have led to new, exciting career prospects for aspiring youth – the craft of the smith had been discovered.

Stone is available almost everywhere and workable varieties are fairly easy to obtain. Not so copper. It is a relatively rare mineral and to detect it the searcher must have some knowledge of ores, and of how to prospect for them. Copper technology must have led to a growing differentiation between the 'haves' and the 'have nots'. Copper-rich regions became wealthy as they realized the potential of their raw material. Long-distance trading inevitably boomed as ores or finished products were distributed. In a world in which some have and some do not, greater opportunity prevailed for social inequality and the exploitation by the élite of their advantages.

Warfare too must have become more commonplace, as people vied with one another for the possession of resources. With the advent of copper technology came the discovery of the metal for which the world still hungers – gold. Oddly enough, gold (which can be worked cold and which is often found in a comparatively pure state) did not figure in the world of Neolithic Man, who had not discovered, or who chose to ignore its glittering delights.

The first smiths
There was no one area where early coppersmiths pioneered their techniques. The belief that copper was first cast in the civilized Near East and, like farming, spread through the rest of the Old World must now be rejected in favour of the theory of an independent invention in at least three separate areas.

Cold-worked copper objects dating from the seventh millennium BC have been found at Çatal Hüyük in Turkey, where copper was probably regarded as a strange type of stone. The discovery that copper can be melted and cast probably did not come about through someone happening to have some lumps of copper ore among the stones of their hearth and seeing them melt as the week's roast spattered above the fire. No domestic hearth was hot enough to melt copper; but the type of pottery kiln used to fire painted pottery may have been. It is not surprising, therefore, that the earliest areas of copper casting are also the regions in which painted pottery was fashionable. A cast copper mace-head datable to around 5000 BC has been found at Can Hassan in Turkey, and it was probably here that copper working was pioneered, for there is an abundant supply of the raw material in a fairly pure state. Soon after the middle of the fifth millennium BC copper casting was fairly commonplace in Mesopotamia.

Meanwhile, copper technology was being developed in the Balkans. Beads of native copper have been found in a cemetery at Cerniça (Romania) dated to around 5000 BC or even earlier. By 4700 BC copper awls and other small cold-worked objects can be found, and by 4000 BC copper casting had been perfected.

It is likely that a third area of early copper metallurgy was the Iberian peninsula. By 3000 BC smiths at Los Millares in Almeria were fashioning cast flat-axes, awls, chisels, saws and knife-daggers, and around the same time crucibles for melting copper and small copper awls attest non-ferrous metallurgy at Vila Nova de São Pedro in central Portugal.

As early as 4000 BC a few copper objects may have been reaching northern Europe from the Balkans. Around 3400 BC new arrivals from the Russian steppe-lands brought copper technology, and for the first time the north European plain had its indigenous production, instead of depending on trade for its supply of copper objects.

The incomers brought about further radical changes. They introduced a new burial rite – single burial under a round earthen mound or barrow. They also probably introduced the wheel, some ancestral form of Indo-European speech, and a new warlike spirit. They made stone battle axes with a central perforation for the haft, and pottery decorated with whipped-cord impressions.

Coincidentally cord impressions were becoming popular among the natives of north-west Europe. As the late Neolithic farmers took over the new lifestyle and many of their characteristics from the incomers from the Steppes, fusion of 'corded' ceramic styles was fairly rapid as well as the adoption of non-ferrous metallurgy.

The Beaker people
The people who are believed to have transmitted copper technology to Britain are known, from their distinctive cord-

impressed pots, as the Beaker folk. This archaeological 'culture' or group of cultures has intrigued prehistorians ever since the beginning of the century, when Lord Abercromby used British beakers to argue that Beaker people from the continent of Europe had invaded Britain in prehistoric times. Beakers have always remained central to European prehistoric studies, and the postulated Beaker folk movements have been taken as a classic example of prehistoric migrations in Europe. Seen as metal-prospectors in search of new sources of ore, they have been invested in archaeological literature with an aura as emotive as that of the Vikings. Despite the research, and the enormous body of evidence for the Beaker people, it has to be admitted that their origins seem almost as obscure as they were in Abercromby's time. There is a growing tendency among prehistorians to believe that contrary to former belief there was more than one origin of the Beaker people. It is certainly possible to distinguish between two main traditions in goods that arguably may reflect two separate groups of peoples.

The first group seems to have originated in northern Europe out of the fusion of the late Neolithic native culture with that of the incomers from the steppe-lands. Characteristic of this Beaker culture are pots decorated with all-over cord impressions. There is little evidence for believing that the users of these All-over Cord beakers actually invaded Britain. However, as a result of contact between these islands and the Low Countries and lower Rhine it would seem that some people in Britain began making beakers with this style of ornament sometime around 3000 BC. Inexplic-

63 All-over Cord beaker (AOC beaker) from Bathgate, West Lothian. This type of beaker developed in northern Europe out of a fusion of native and intrusive ceramic styles, but its appearance in Britain does not seem to be due to invasion. Early third millennium BC

ably, radio-carbon dates for some of the finds of All-over Cord beaker sherds in Britain and Ireland are as early, if not earlier, than the available dates for those on the Continent: this problem has not been resolved.

The users of the second type of beaker (Maritime beaker) seem to have spread along the western coast of Spain and France from their original homelands in Iberia. These Maritime Beaker folk spread progressively northwards until they mixed with the All-over Cord Beaker people in the Rhineland and Low Countries. The result seems to have been hybrid types of Beaker pottery. From around 2500 BC Maritime and other beakers were introduced to Britain as a result of protracted immigrations. These gave rise under local stimulus to regional types.

There can be no doubt that the number of Beaker immigrants was appreciable. This can be demonstrated because Beaker people were of different physical type from the native Neolithic stock. The skeletons from middle Neolithic chambered tombs and long barrows are of gracile individuals with dolichocephalic (i.e. long) skulls. Beaker folk in contrast are found in round barrows – their skeletons are more robust and brachycephalic (i.e. with round skulls). The old saying 'long skulls long barrows; round skulls round barrows' in general is as true now as it was when Thurnam was studying skulls in 1871 and Abercromby was writing in 1912.

The Beaker folk mixed fairly easily and peacefully with the native inhabitants. Beaker pottery is frequently found in megalithic chambered tombs, and beaker association with many of the native ritual monuments of late Neolithic

64 A Maritime or Bell beaker, from Fingask, Perthshire, decorated with chevron patterns inlaid with white paint. Such beakers seem to have spread from Iberia along the Atlantic coast, and to have been introduced to Britain by incomers around 2500 BC. These people, the Beaker folk, introduced single inhumation burial and copper technology. Local types of beaker evolved out of imported Maritime styles

143

Britain is apparent. In their flint-work they took over some of the traditions of local Neolithic communities, and in turn local Neolithic pottery was influenced by Beaker styles. The fact that gracile dolichocephalic skeletons have been found in Beaker-style burials indicates that some of the native population adopted a Beaker lifestyle.

The Beaker people did not only introduce copper working and new ceramics – they made some changes in farming. They began a new and vigorous phase of forest clearance,

65 This Short-necked beaker was found at Edzell, Angus, and is a type which was current in northern Britain

and as a result of their activities many areas were irreversibly turned to grassland and heath. They continued to grow all the crops already established, but showed a preference for barley (to make alcoholic beverages to quaff from their beakers?) and also grew bread wheat. Barley may have had a double advantage in that surplus could be used for fodder. They also seem to have improved livestock.

They may have introduced a new breed of cattle, *bos longifrons* – the Beaker people were cowmen. They domesticated the horse, though probably for meat rather than for riding or draught. Though there is no evidence so far for this in Britain, domesticated horses are known from Beaker sites in Ireland.

The Beaker people introduced a variety of new types of object into Britain. They made characteristic flint arrowheads of barbed and tanged form (in contrast to the leaf-shaped or transverse arrow heads of the native Neolithic inhabitants), and they made copper tanged and rivetted knives, awls, thick-butted axes and the occasional pin for fastening their clothing.

Irish gold reserves were exploited, and the Beaker people made ornate gold necklets known to archaeologists as lunulae, the designs of which sometimes seem to follow those on Beaker pottery. They also produced less accomplished gold basket-shaped earrings and objects known as sun-discs – gold ornaments which may reflect the interest in a sun-cult or which may have been badges of office. They traded quite far afield, and not only Irish gold but Irish copper axes may have been sold over wide areas. From the Continent jade axes were still marketed as well as lava from the Niedermendig quarries in Germany. These stone works were incidentally still supplying querns to Anglo-Saxon England nearly 3,000 years later. Amber, a fossil resin much admired in prehistoric times, was traded too in the form of beads, and worked jet and shale found their way on to the market. V-perforated jet buttons often turn up in Beaker burials, as occasionally do stone wrist-guards for archers. Later Beaker societies seem to have been familiar with arsenical copper alloys, and occasionally even used tin bronze.

Some Beaker burials shed interesting side-lights on their world. A pathetic note is struck by a barrow excavated on Normanton Down in Wiltshire. No less than eleven burials were found within it, nearly all of children, buried separately or in pairs. The barrow was surrounded by a double ditch, and in the entrance gap through the inner ditch were laid the bodies of a nine-year-old child and a baby of no more than one or two months. To accompany the child was a normal sized beaker, but the baby was given a tiny beaker specially made for it. The barrow was perhaps constructed to receive the bodies of those who had died in an epidemic. In the same county near Amesbury a leather-worker's grave was found, furnished with a cup and an assortment of tools. A wooden tool was in his hand and a

66 Neatly worked barbed and tanged arrowheads such as these were used by the Beaker folk. Barbed and tanged flint arrows remained popular during the first part of the Bronze Age

0   1   2   3 cm

pointed wooden board had been laid over his body. Some late handled beakers from East Anglia are clearly representations in pottery of wooden mugs – the decoration on the base imitates the grain of the wood. Some people who could not afford copper daggers had to make do with second best – flint imitations of them. These would not have been very effective when stuck into wooden handles, and may have been for ornament or ritual rather than use. A bone copy of a handled copper dagger has been found in the London area.

67 Gold lunula, Auchentaggart, Sanquhar, Dumfriesshire. These neck-ornaments were produced by the Beaker people, and in their engraved decoration often use motifs borrowed from Beaker pottery

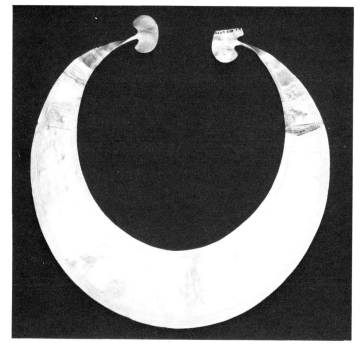

A Beaker burial from Crichel Down, Dorset, not only displayed a spinal deformity, but also showed evidence of having died under the knife. A surgeon had attempted to trepan the man's skull, and although he had cut a huge roundel out very neatly, he had been rather ambitious in his endeavours.

Beaker settlements are not often found by excavators, but from those that have been excavated it is apparent that the Beaker people lived in single-family houses, widely dispersed rather than in villages. Their homes were circular or more rarely rectilinear, and were built either of single posts or of posts set in bedding trenches. At Belle Tout, Sussex, a group of Beaker houses was found inside a defensive enclosure, defined by a bank and ditch.

Despite the changes wrought by the Beaker people, the 'copper age' had had little real impact upon society and it was not until the working of bronze was introduced that the advantages and disadvantages of metal-using societies were apparent.

The sources (the Age of Bronze)

In Britain the Bronze Age is distinguished by having left very uneven evidence. Most of the remains are of graves – Bronze Age archaeology centres around barrow types and their contents (which are all too often merely urns contain-

68 Detail of the terminal of a lunula from Ireland, showing the Beaker style of ornament (compare this with plate 64)

ing the ashes of the dead and little else). As the age wore on, bronze tools, weapons and ornaments became progressively common and frequently turn up in hoards. Many of these were the stock-in-trade collections of scrap metal of travelling smiths who for some reason or other buried their

147

goods and never retrieved them. In the middle and especially the late period of the Bronze Age much of the work of the prehistorian has been connected with the study and classification of this type of metal-work from hoards. Throughout the period the study of pottery has been important as a source of information. Settlements are few and mostly belong to the second half of the Bronze Age. Accordingly relatively little is known about everyday life in Bronze Age Britain.

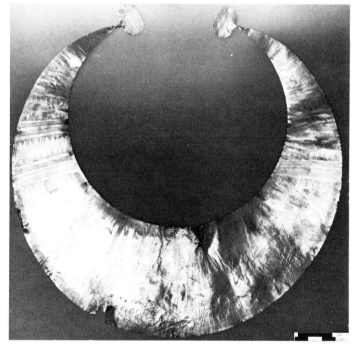

69 Lunula from Ayr or Lanark, Scotland, with elaborate geometric ornament

In contrast much is known about the ritual monuments of the time. The stone circles and henges that were a feature of the late Neolithic continued in use. Standing stones were apparently erected and many burials are associated with Bronze Age ritual sites. In the Highland areas strange carvings are found but cannot be explained – the most distinctive are the 'cup and ring' marks.

Although conventionally the Bronze Age is divided into early, middle and late phases, with the increase in knowledge it has become more fashionable to refer only to an earlier and a later period. The divide is seen as coming around 1400 BC. During the earlier Bronze Age (c. 2000–1400 BC) the dead were laid to rest with flat copper axes, awls and copper daggers, from which evolved various dagger types. During the early period a rich gold-using aristocracy flourished in the south-west – the Wessex culture. This had far-flung links with the Continent. There are also a few hints that stock-rearing became more important during the early Bronze Age than it had been in the Neolithic period. It was during this time that the monument of Stonehenge as we think of it today was completed.

The break around 1400 BC was heralded by a change in the weather, which became cooler and wetter so that old settlements were gradually abandoned. The ancient types

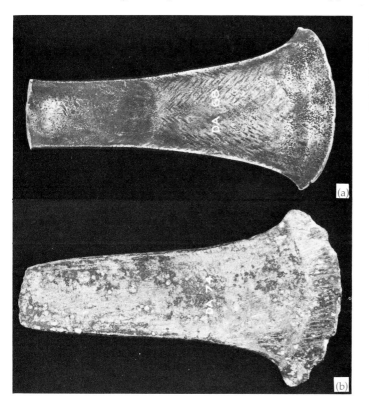

70 (a) and (b) Cast flat axes from Harlaw Muir, Innerleithen, Peeblesshire, decorated with incised linear patterns. These were cast in open moulds, and are among the earliest products of smiths in Britain

of ritual site – stone circles, burial mounds and henges – went out of use. A new pattern of settlement similar to that of the Iron Age was established – round timber huts, systems of irregular fields, and storage pits, for example, became commonplace.

Hill-forts began to make their appearance and society in general seems to have become more warlike. There were many innovations and modifications made to various weapons.

After about the tenth century BC new traditions accelerated. A new alloy – lead bronze – appeared in Britain. Mass production of bronze was a feature of the age. By the eighth century the new trends began to catch on in the north and west. From this time on there was something of an 'Industrial Revolution' with a much wider range of products available for the consumer. During the late Bronze Age also, Britain was vulnerable to outside stimulus after centuries of indigenous development. In this period, for a brief time, the area seems to have been caught up in a 'Common Market' of Atlantic coastal trade in which buckets and cauldrons, axes and other objects were exchanged, some with origins ultimately in Mediterranean lands.

Burial rite in the early Bronze Age

In the early Bronze Age cremation became the fashion. Cremation burials of the early Bronze Age were interred in large coarse pots known to archaeologists as cinerary urns. These fall into different groups. One of the largest series

71 Overhanging-rim urn, found in a barrow on Stockbridge Down, Hants. It was inverted over a secondary cremation, and was found along with a segmented faience bead imported from the Mediterranean and a bronze awl. Early Bronze Age. Such pots were used for cremations. Height: 39.37 cm

comprises the collared urns. These show clear Neolithic antecedents, with perhaps some influence from late beakers. The cremating users of cinerary urns were staunch adherents to Neolithic values. They sometimes used old henges as their burial grounds, or, if a suitable local example was unavailable, they would build a new one, as happened for example at Loanhead of Daviot, Aberdeenshire. They also used a variety of henge-like enclosures as specially constructed graveyards.

Those who considered inhumation a more acceptable method of disposing of their deceased loved ones usually buried them with one of the many popular styles of 'food vessel'. These were similarly derived from late Neolithic styles and shapes, of which the main ones were vases and bowls. Vases were popular in England, bowls in Ireland, and both were favoured in Scotland. The influence of Grooved ware (see p. 101) can be detected in many of the food vessels, particularly in the elaborate series of ridged buckets and vases. As cremation caught on generally, some users of food vessels took it up, making special 'enlarged food vessels' to contain the ashes.

Food vessel burial customs tended to follow those of the later Beaker folk. In the highland zone bodies were laid in cists composed of stone slabs; in the lowland parts of the country where there was more soil (and wood for making coffins?) burials were laid in holes dug in the ground. South of the Tees burials were under barrows, north of it they tended to be in flat, unmarked cemeteries.

While the different types of early Bronze Age pots were being used, Beaker pottery continued. From this is it

72 (left) Encrusted urn, Ovingham, Northumberland. Found inverted over a cremation adjacent to four cists, two with cremations, and an enlarged food vessel. Encrusted urns were a specialized type of food vessel (see plate 73), current in northern Britain in the first part of the Bronze Age. Height: 38.1 cm

73 (right) Fine example of a food vessel of the early Bronze Age, of a type known as a 'Yorkshire vase'. The decoration, which perhaps imitates basketry, owes something to the Peterborough tradition of later Neolithic pottery (compare with plate 35)

151

possible to infer that the Beaker people were some kind of social élite, with their own funerary monuments and traditions, and the food vessel users were lesser mortals in the same social hierarchy, who surreptitiously inserted their burials into the funerary monuments of their superiors? Certainly others seem to have been strongly influenced by Beaker traditions and taste. The users of cinerary urns, however, seem to have been more independent of spirit: good old Neolithic stock who built their own funerary monuments when necessary, but were not averse to placing a burial in someone else's barrow.

Barrows and barrow-diggers

> Barrow digging is somewhat like bottom fishing [wrote Rooke Pennington, a Bolton solicitor who went in for the former occupation in his spare time in the 1870s]. There is plenty of fun and excitement when you are fairly in for a good thing . . . but when work is hard and results small, you lie down and smoke your pipe and watch your comrades, and begin to think profanely of the memory of the Prehistoric niggards. . . . Sometimes you meet with a regular 'sell', as though some Neolithic humorist had prepared some elaborate practical joke for your especial benefit.

It is thanks to such indefatigable nineteenth-century barrow-diggers that the museum cases of provincial Britain are filled with 'sad sepulchral urns' and the bits and pieces that were recovered from countless Bronze Age barrows the length and breadth of the land. Weather was no obstacle. J. R. Mortimer at Painsthorpe (Yorkshire) chronicled that 'the weather was so hot that at times we had to protect ourselves from the scorching sun by sheltering under our conveyance, whilst a servant mowing thistles in the same field divested himself of all clothing, save his shirt and boots', while at Aldro he reported 'there was a heavy fall of snow . . . causing our work to be conducted under adverse conditions'. Mortimer also had to contend with visitors, including on one occasion seventeen onlookers, among them six doctors and a parson. The Peakland digger Thomas Bateman was even less lucky with onlookers – they openly 'abstracted' bones and other objects from his trenches at Steep Low (Derbyshire), and crowded so close that more than one of them fell into his cutting. Eventually he was forced to give up until 'the march of civilization shall have penetrated these benighted regions'. Still, life could have been worse! On one of Bateman's excavations the party was refreshed fairly adequately. It was thought that digging might be hungry work,

So ham, veal, rabbits, lamb, at once were thrust
With varied condiments beneath a crust.

and at mid-day

Pie of rabbits – tongue and chine –
Leg of poultry – cheek of swine –
Pickled salmon – onion – mango –
Down the throat fast as they can go.
Brandy and beer
Bring up the rear.
(S. Isaacson, *Barrow Digging by a Barrow Knight*, 1845)

Bronze Age burial sites, like their Neolithic predecessors, come in all shapes and sizes. Burials can be found under barrows of different shapes, in stone circles, or within other circles which lack the standing stones. The ritual that was attendant on their construction was varied, and sheds some insight into the twilight world of Bronze Age death. Now and again we can detect something which has a poignancy for modern minds. At Ashgrove in Fife a warrior burial was covered with a mass of leaves. A grieving relative had laid on the corpse some lime and meadow-sweet before it was confined to the darkness, and sphagnum moss on the body may have been some kind of surgical dressing. A more recent suggestion, however, is that this is the remains of a beaker filled with mead that was inadvertently upset over the body!

No book on early prehistoric Britain would be complete without reference to some of the horror stories that can be constructed. The most horrid concern the sacrifice of infants. Evidence for this comes from a series of Bronze Age burials in Wales, notably from the Brenig Valley where a series of barrows were opened in 1976. The most complex, prosaically known as Brenig 45, had a secondary burial set in the side. When the urn was lifted it was found to contain not the customary ashes but the earbones and two molar crowns

74 Reconstruction of a hafted dagger from Ashgrove, Fife, of the early Bronze Age. The hilt plates were of horn, with an ivory pommel, and it was found in the remains of a leather sheath. Associated with the burial was a beaker

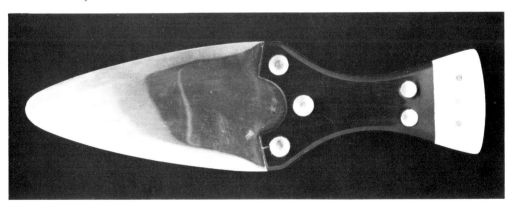

of an infant. Were this unique, little might be made of it, but in Anglesey two other occurrences have been noted. At Bedd Branwen three pairs of petrous temporal bones from newborn babies were found burnt. At Triorweth on the same island the earbones of a six-year-old child came to light. All the other bones in each case were absent: these were no ordinary child burials. As the earbones are deeply embedded in the brain, they could not have been retrieved unless the brains had been ripped out. The bones may have served as symbols of the brain, which may have been eaten. There are hints too that the secondary burials found in some barrows may have been the victims of suttee – women buried to accompany their men to the afterlife, or in some cases the sacrifice of slaves.

Charcoal and burning suggest that the sites were sometimes ritually fumigated. Grains of barley on a sherd of pottery from a barrow in the Yorkshire Wolds suggest that offerings of grain were occasionally made. At Sutton, Glamorgan, the earth around a barrow was compacted, apparently as a result of dancers circling it. Sometimes ritual pits have been found under barrows; possibly these were intended to contain offerings to the underworld. Some barrows seem to have been built over the funeral pyre – one yielded the burnt remains of oak (the usual fuel), holly, willow and purging buckthorn – a particularly good mixture for burning well. Stone rings are sometimes found within barrows, or sometimes retaining them. Circles of stakes are also found under barrows, or around them, as are concealed ditches. Timber mortuary houses have been found under barrows, and can be square, rectangular or round. Some are gabled (for example at Wrangworthy Cross in Devon) and

75 Bronze Age round barrow during excavation at Breach Farm, Llanblethian, Glamorgan. This remarkable barrow shows connections with the Wessex culture of southern England. Notice the retaining wall, the turfs visible in the section, and the central burial deposit. The burial was associated with a biconical pygmy cup and axe probably imported from Wessex, as well as typically 'Wessex' daggers

recall the type of structure underlying Wayland's Smithy (see pp. 126–8). A stone was sometimes set on top of a barrow. Potsherds, burnt flint, and earth apparently from domestic floors have all been found in the makeup of barrows. All in all the structures and finds indicate a diversity of ritual associated with burial in Bronze Age Britain.

Cup and ring marks

Megalithic art of the type found in the tombs of the Boyne valley and in Anglesey was short-lived (pp. 129–30) and the Bronze Age had its own series of mysterious carvings – the cup and ring marks. The term is derived from the most characteristic symbol, a hollow or 'cup' contained within a pecked 'ring', or series of concentric rings. The cup and ring marks seem to originate in the Neolithic – the earliest recorded example comes from under an earthen long barrow dated to 3240 BC – but the great majority belong to the second millennium BC. As well as the cup and ring symbols there are spirals, lozenges, hands and feet, axes, 'wheels', 'eyebrows' and patterns that look remarkably like letters. They are particularly common on the stones of the cists that contain Bronze Age burials, but they are also found on standing stones and on rock outcrops through most of

76 Cup and ring markings on a rock face in Argyll. The precise function of these carvings is unknown – they are the successors of 'passage grave art' and are often found associated with the stones of burial cists, hence their other name of 'single grave art'

the Highland Zone of Britain. They have been found on stones incorporated into Iron Age structures, but these may have already existed on the material used by chance by the later builders.

Current opinion favours the view that 'single grave art', as it is called, originated in Britain and Ireland out of earlier Boyne valley 'passage grave art', and that from northern Britain it may have spread to other areas on the Continent, such as Iberia, perhaps as a result of Britain's overseas trade.

77 Engraved examples of 'single grave art' on a stone from Lamancha, Peeblesshire. Early Bronze Age

The interpretation of the 'single grave art' has foxed experts. One mathematician, Professor Alexander Thom, believes that the cup and ring marks have diameters in multiples of a unit which he has termed the 'megalithic inch'. It has been suggested that some are solar symbols, connected with a sky cult, perhaps the same cult that led to the association of axes and henges. Carvings of hands and feet may be indications of divinity or royal status, though in some societies these have been symbols of death, for example in the Roman Empire. A suggestion has also been made that they are not religious, but simply prospectors' symbols!

Stone circles

Avebury henge has survived as a centre of pagan ritual into modern times. In the nineteenth century children danced round a maypole there, where three centuries previously a similar maypole had been the focus for celebrations of a less innocent kind. 'And then fall they to daunce about it, like as the heathen people did at the dedication of the Idols,' Stubbs wrote in the sixteenth century about the maypole, 'I have heard it creditably reported . . . that of fortie, three-score or a hundred maidens going to the wood overnight, there have been scaresly the third part returned home undefiled.'

In 1773 Dr Johnson visited a stone circle near Inverness. 'To go and see one druidical temple is only to see that it is nothing, for there is neither art nor power in it, and seeing

one is quite enough.' However much some of us might secretly agree with the learned gentleman, modern opinion in general differs from his. Perhaps surprisingly, too, the current modern view is that there is more art in them than even the most imaginative contemporaries of the eighteenth century wit could have conjured up.

Stone circles are the most evocative prehistoric monuments in Britain. Jagged as giants' teeth they stand on moorland and arable land in both highland and lowland. Legends and moss cling to them alike and they are still claimed to possess miraculous powers. Stone circles have been claimed as being part of a vast telepathic network of obscure purpose, as the 'batteries' that are charged with ancient knowledge and power, as the work of Martians (the Beaker people were believed by one archaeologist to have come from Mars), and as the work of Egyptian colonists. Egyptians and druids have both been canvassed along with Danes and Romans as the builders of Stonehenge. One recent writer thought that though originally Egyptian, Stonehenge was redesigned by Delian Greeks who dedi-

78 A stone circle viewed through the eyes of a seven-teenth-century antiquary. An engraving by Kip of the Roll-right Stones, Oxfordshire, from the 1695 edition of Camden's *Britannia*

cated it to Apollo. One person has ventured the opinion that Stonehenge was one of the five great cities of Britain, and another that it was built by a man called Gwlyddin, which can be translated as, apparently, 'Hero, foremost expert of the Grey Stones'. Medieval writers thought Stonehenge was the work of Merlin. Some have considered it the labour of the Phoenicians. Certain archaeologists have claimed it to be designed by an architect from Mycenae in Greece.

First, then, the basic facts. Half the battle is won if stone circles and standing stones are viewed simply as part of a complex series of ritual monuments in Neolithic and Bronze Age Britain, of which the causewayed camps and later the henge monuments were all part and parcel. Over 900 stone circles either exist in Britain, or survived long enough to be recorded. The earliest is that of Newgrange in Ireland, where a circle surrounded the megalithic passage grave. It has been dated to 3300 BC. The latest is a circle at Scone, Perthshire, dated to around 1500 BC. Most were built after 2500 BC.

Stone circles fall into two main families. *Open circles* have no pits or other features inside them and *funerary circles* contain burials. Not all 'true' circles, they can be flattened rings, ellipses, egg-shaped, or complex (laid out according to advanced geometry). 'Four-posters' are 'circles' of four stones, which cannot validly be grouped with the above.

79 Silhouetted against the sky, the stones of Callanish, Lewis, epitomize the mystery that surrounds the stone circles of the Bronze Age. Callanish is one of the finest of the stone circles in Britain, and also one of the most complex. An avenue 82.3m long marked out by 19 standing stones terminates in a circle 11.3m in diameter, composed of 13 stones, which extend on either side into a cross row of 4 stones. Opposite the first avenue is a shorter, second one of 6 stones. Adjacent are burial mounds, and a ruined chambered tomb stands in the centre

Most rings, however, were true circles, which are of course the easiest to lay out – 600 true circles are known in Britain, as opposed to 150 flattened circles, the next most common group. Stone circles appear to have been laid out using a measurement known as the 'Megalithic Yard' – 0.829m. Some stone circles have diameters of up to 113m, the smallest are less than 3m in diameter. Some circles are contained within henges (p. 114). Some, such as the Kennet Avenue at Avebury or the line at Callanish in Lewis have associated alignments of stones. Some contain earlier chambered tombs. Some have a central standing stone, some have the stone set within a rubble bank. A few concentric circles are known. Individual stones vary in height – the highest of the stones at the Stones of Stenness in Orkney is 5.2m – those at Stonehenge average only 4.1m.

Thus far we are on fairly firm ground. The next two questions – 'how did stone circles evolve?' and 'what was their function?' take us into deeper water.

The easier to answer of the two questions concerns origins. Stone circles appear to be closely related to henges, and probably descend from them. Areas where large stone circles are found, usually also have henges. The very largest stone circles are never far away from henge monuments, and in areas where there are no henges the stone circles that are found are both late and small. Some henges have stone circles within them – at Avebury henge and circle appear to be contemporary. In other cases the circle may have been added to an existing henge. This was the case at Stonehenge, and at Cairnpapple in West Lothian.

80 The Ring of Brodgar, Orkney. One of the largest stone circles in Britain, there are 27 of the original 60 stones enclosing an area 109.7m in diameter. One stone in the circle stands 4.6m high. Adjacent is the Stenness Circle, joined to Brodgar by a 'processional way' of single standing stones across the isthmus that separates Loch Stenness and Loch of Harray. The whole complex, with Maes Howe and the scatter of Bronze Age round barrows, recalls Avebury or Stonehenge

Why were stones erected? Some may be translations into stone of timber posts. Wooden structures such as those at Woodhenge and Durrington Walls (p. 114) appear to have been buildings. Settings of individual posts like stone circles have been found in a henge at Arminghall in Norfolk and freestanding at Caerloggas in Cornwall. The Arminghall setting was horseshoe-shaped, that at Caerloggas a full circle. A circle of single wooden posts also seems to have preceded the stone circle at Croft Moraig, Perthshire, where again the circle was horseshoe-shaped. There is no certain proof, however, that stone circles were generally preceded by timber ones, and it is quite possible that timber and stone were alternatives dependent on availability of material.

The occurrence of burials within stone circles raises the question of whether funeral monuments may have contributed to their development. Kerbs of stones frequently surround the passage graves of the Boyne valley in Ireland, and a similar kerb can be seen round the Boyne-style tomb of Bryn Celli Ddu in Anglesey. Some of the Boyne tombs' kerbstones are decorated with 'passage grave art', and it is noteworthy that the Bronze Age equivalent, cup and ring

81 Avebury, Wiltshire, from the air. This complex monument has the remains of subsidiary circles within the main one, which stands inside a henge monument. Notice the Kennet Avenue – a processional way of parallel lines of stones leading towards the top left-hand corner of the picture, followed by the line of the modern road. This terminated in the 'Sanctuary' on Overton hill. Notice also the crop-marks of ploughed-out barrows in the field adjacent (*top centre*)

marks, are found on some Bronze Age standing stones. It is possible that the building of a stone ring preceded the erection of some passage graves. In later times stone circles seem to have been 'grafted on' to late chambered tombs, for example in the Clava group of tombs in Inverness-shire. Certainly later stone circles were frequently used for burials, and at Cairnpapple a burial mound was erected in the Bronze Age within a stone circle. In parts of western Britain stone circles and burial mounds were combined, to produce various funerary monuments such as 'cairn-circles' and 'kerb-cairns'.

The function of stone circles and standing stones can be summarized under two heads. First, there is the astronomical function that has been postulated for them, and second there are the other ritual usages that have been inferred.

It has already been demonstrated (p. 117) that early henge monuments may reflect the astronomical knowledge of their builders. It would logically follow that stone circles and standing stones do likewise. In fact, stone circles are not ideal monuments for astronomical observation. As one expert has pointed out, stones providing an alignment or a

82 Avebury, Wiltshire. Some of the stones round the lip of the henge ditch

horseshoe of monoliths for calderical calculation would be more useful. The problems involved in proving astronomical function are enormous, since it is difficult to ascertain the alignments that were operative at the time the circles were erected. Furthermore, it is not always certain that the stones are now in exactly their original positions or that all are still present. Nevertheless, there is a sufficient body of evidence to suggest strongly that astronomical observation was one, if not the most important, function of many stone circles.

83 Long Meg and her Daughters, a romantically sited circle of standing stones above Penrith, Cumbria, typical of the smaller stone circles of Bronze Age Britain

The later, smaller circles show more signs of having been used for this purpose than the early, larger ones. Early stone circles seem to have orientations within them on the sun's or moon's main positions, or on major stars. Observations from these were probably integral to the planning of seasonal festivals. Such ceremonies are a fundamental part of European tradition. Down to medieval times, festivals were held in spring and at midsummer and, in north-west Europe, at Hallowe'en (the Celtic Samain) and May Day (Celtic Beltane).

It is possible to infer that rituals were associated with henges and causewayed camps. Stone circles seem to be associated ritually with stone axes, for example. A broken axe was found in a pit at Grey Croft circle in Cumbria and axes are carved at Stonehenge. Considerable numbers of axes have been found near the Avebury and Brodgar circles. Stone axes seem to have been associated with the sun and a sun cult. Perhaps they were connected with a sky god. Even today axes are considered symbols of fertility in Germany, and evidence for axes as pagan symbols can be found all over north-west Europe. In western England even in recent times stone axes were considered to be thunderbolts, and some were placed in cattle troughs to protect the beasts from ill-health.

Fertility was probably central to the rituals performed at stone circles. The phallic shape of the stones themselves is

obvious, and it is hardly surprising that they were regarded as ensuring fertility in recent historic times. The central standing stone of some circles is particularly likely to have been a focus for ritual in this connection.

Dancing may well have been one of the activities of the circle builders. Some tradition of dancing within stone circles is perhaps preserved in folklore – many rings are supposedly maidens who were petrified for dancing on a Sunday. The Merry Maidens in Cornwall is one such example. At Stanton Drew in Somerset the stones are supposedly a wedding party transformed for the same reason.

At this point the discussion of stone circles tends to pass almost imperceptibly into the realms of fantasy. There is an impelling urge to start considering in general prehistoric European religion and its survivals, drawing from folklore, superstition, pagan survivals documented in literature, later archaeological evidence, and, if the scholar has a mind to it,

84 Stone circles may not always be what they seem. This stone circle formed the kerb of a burial cairn since robbed out at Temple Wood, Argyll – the stone cist in the centre once contained a Bronze Age cremation burial

examples of dark doings in circles in the far corners of the globe at various times to the present day. Such speculations serve merely to show us just how limited the archaeological evidence is in connection with ritual and belief and just how many possible interpretations can be made from the same meagre clues.

One last observation can be made. When the religion of the Iron Age Celts is considered carefully it shows many features that are strangely similar to those of Neolithic and Bronze Age belief, as far as can be reasonably inferred from archaeology. Briefly, survivals were the concept of a ritual circle, the re-use of many earlier ritual sites, the pattern of festivals, the votive pots, the axe symbols. Scholars have long mocked the romantics who still speak of Stonehenge as a druid temple and the re-founded druid order which practises its ceremonials there at midsummer. Yet there is growing evidence that the Celtic religion of the druids stemmed from something much older, something which was a part of prehistoric European beliefs. Between the stone circle builders and the druids there was no major wave of incomers in the British Isles. It could therefore be claimed with some validity that Stonehenge was indeed built by Bronze Age 'druids'. The wheel of prehistoric studies seems to have come full circle from the time of Stukeley.

The culmination of Stonehenge

Around 2150 BC Stonehenge (see Plate 85) was once again the scene of intense activity. The objective was the building of concentric circles of stones, 26.2m and 22.6m in diameter, which was accompanied by the construction of a 2.8km-long avenue from the river Avon to the henge. The entrance was widened to accommodate the huge stones, and we can imagine some landing-stage by the river where the 82 huge, 4-ton blocks (mainly of dolerite) were disembarked for the last short leg of their 200-mile journey. For these, the 'bluestones' of Stonehenge, had been transported from Carn Meini in the Prescelly mountains of south-west Wales.

It is always assumed that the stones were transported and erected without the aid of the wheel – instead they were carried by waterway on canoes and then dragged overland on sledges on rollers. On site, it is assumed they were hoisted up with levers and with the possible aid of ramps or cradles. There is, however, no concrete reason for believing that the builders of Stonehenge were not in possession of the wheel, and it is not impossible that they had pulleys. Evidence points to the wheel being brought to Europe by the people who also introduced the rite of single-grave burial.

Several solid (i.e. non-spoked) wheels have been found in the Netherlands, in one case closely associated with a corduroy road similar to those in the Somerset Levels; these have been dated to around 2500 BC or even slightly earlier. Wheels could easily have been introduced by the Beaker people, and the fact that none have been found is not surprising, since they would have been made of wood and thus be unlikely to survive. Pulleys too, were apparently known in the later Bronze Age, for they had almost certainly been employed in the construction of the Wilsford shaft (p. 110).

But whatever method of construction was used, the bluestone circle of Stonehenge remained unfinished. The plan was changed and the builders began erecting the famous circle of sarsen stones around the interior of the henge. The bluestone rings were dismantled and presumably stored near the site, and then instead forty sarsen uprights were hoisted into position and joined by thirty-five lintels, the stones this time being transported from the Marlborough Downs about 24km to the north. The arrangement of this phase (known as Stonehenge IIIa), involved an outer circle of 30 uprights and lintels, and an inner horseshoe of five free-standing settings of trilithons, the Station Stones, Slaughter Stone and its companion.

This temple was technically very sophisticated. The lintels have sockets which fit on to projecting knobs on the top of the uprights. Many of the uprights and lintels are carefully dressed, and each of the lintels in the main circle has a tongue and a groove at opposite ends to link it with the next one and strengthen the circle. This technique was probably derived from woodworking, and it strongly suggests that Stonehenge is a stone version of a type of timber circle. The geometry of this phase of construction is very sophisticated.

Around the time this sarsen monument was put up the bluestones were re-erected in a new monument elsewhere. The site has not been discovered and its existence has been inferred. If this sounds somewhat extraordinary at first, it is explained by the fact that this putative second site was apparently dismantled and the boulders brought back once more to Stonehenge. Various traces of re-working can be seen on the stones thus returned. For example, the second putative site seems to have been erected in trilithons, since there is clear evidence that knobs for taking the lintels have been removed from some of the stones now at Stonehenge. After the dismantling, the stones were to be re-erected in a double circle at Stonehenge or more probably in a spiral outside the sarsen circle. The holes known as the Y and Z holes were partly dug and then abandoned. Instead the final layout adopted was the one that is visible today (Stonehenge IIIc) with the inner circle and horseshoe of bluestones within the sarsen monument.

Radio-carbon dates are available for Stonehenge IIIa which indicate that it was erected around 2100 BC. The transition between the abandoned bluestone spiral (IIIb) and the finished monument (IIIc) has been assigned to around 1490 BC.

Stonehenge is unique – one of the most remarkable structures of perhistoric Europe. It is hardly surprising that at the time of its final construction Wessex was the home of a rich aristocracy.

The gold of Wessex

Stonehenge in its final phase was completed at a time when Wessex was dominated by a powerful group of war-lords. For many decades active debate has surrounded the nature of what has rather prosaically been called the 'Wessex culture'. In fact there is no such thing as a Wessex culture, only a series of rich Wessex graves, the last resting places of the war-lords and their womenfolk who were laid to rest during the period 1800–1400 BC. As far as can be ascertained, the ordinary inhabitants of early Bronze Age Wessex lived out their lives in much the same way that they had done for centuries, while their overlords grew rich and powerful and organized a network of trade on a scale hitherto unknown in prehistoric Britain.

The earliest of the rich Wessex graves contain fine gold-work which has echoes of a Beaker past, and which has recently been shown to have been the product of a single *atelier* or even craftsman working around 1800 BC. His masterpieces can be seen at their best in the grave found in Bush Barrow, Wiltshire, in 1808, not far from Stonehenge. The chief was laid extended on his back, a lozenge of sheet gold on his chest, two daggers to his right with a gold scabbard hook and a small gold lozenge that had once been attached to some garment. Nearby were the remains of a sceptre, its shaft decorated with carved zig-zag bone mounts, its head of polished stone. A copper axe lay by his right shoulder. One of the daggers had its hilt inlaid with several thousand tiny gold pins, and this device, along with the style of the sceptre mounts, betrays Breton connections.

The Bush Barrow master may have been responsible for the fine gold-work found in other Wiltshire barrows, at

86 Gold ornaments from the rich Wessex chieftain's burial at Bush Barrow, near Stonehenge, Wilts. The large gold plate (21.6 cm across) lay on the man's chest, and presumably was sewn on to a garment. To the right is the gold plate from a belt hook, and beneath it another plate presumably attached to his clothes. Such objects attest the wealth of the aristocracy of early Bronze Age Wessex

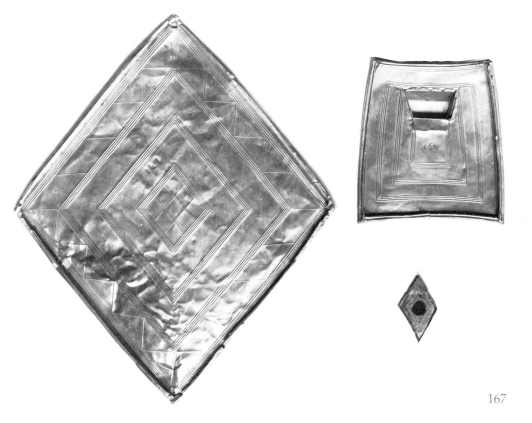

87 Group of finds from a Wessex burial at Snowshill, Gloucestershire. The ogival dagger on the top is a type known from this find as a 'Snowshill' dagger (length: 21.33 cm). The object on the left is a spearhead – both have what the Victorians pictur-esquely called 'blood grooves'. The pin (*right, centre*) is a mid-European crutch-headed type, clearly an import. The stone battle axe is typical of 'Wessex' burials

Manton, Upton Lovell, Clandon Barrow and grave 8 at Wilsford. The Manton barrow was heaped up over the body of an old woman who was buried with a necklace of beads of Dorset shale, an amber disc bound with gold, a tiny pendant in the shape of a halberd and a dagger. The Upton Lovell barrow contained a gold plate, amber necklace, a shale button with gold covering, a dagger, a bodkin, hollow gold beads and two gold cones.

The translucent, glowing amber so prized by the Wessex aristocrats was fashioned into such masterpieces as the cup from Hove, Sussex, or the elaborately strung multi-strand necklaces with spacer plates on which the design of the string was picked out in dots, where it would have shown through. These necklaces, fashioned from East Anglian or Baltic amber, were traded far beyond the realms of Wessex. One was found in a Mycenaean shaft grave of the sixteenth

88 Stone battle axes were introduced to Britain by the Beaker folk, who had acquired the idea of using them from incomers in northern Europe known as the Single-grave Battle-axe people (from whom they acquired other traits such as single-grave burial). Various types of battle axe evolved in early Bronze Age Britain – some, such as that from Snowshill, were distinc-tively boat-shaped. This one is another type, with hammer-like ends. Whether they were actually battle axes is open to question – the name is once again an antiquarian whimsy

century BC in Greece, others in various Mycenaean contexts down to the fourteenth century BC, for example, at Kakovatos in Greece. Spacer plates from similar necklaces can be used to pick out the route they travelled through Europe, examples turning up at places such as Mehrstetten in southern Germany.

The extent of Wessex connections with the Mycenaean world has been hotly debated for almost as long as the Wessex culture has been known. The idea that merchants

89 The Rillaton Cup. This superb gold cup, 8.9 cm high, was found in a barrow at Rillaton, Cornwall. It shows features in common with Mycenaean gold-work, and is fashioned from a single lump of gold, its handle made from a separate piece attached by gold rivets and washers. It is said that Edward VII kept his collar studs in it for a while. Such cups are very rare in Europe – there is one from Fritzdorf in Germany. It could be either a Mediterranean import or a native copy. Height: 8.38 cm

from an ancient Mediterranean civilization should be interested in doing deals with far-off Britain is fascinating and at once evokes pictures of swarthy, exotically dressed Greeks haggling with sign-language over a load of amber or pile of copper daggers. In fact it cannot be ascertained whether Mycenaean merchants ever came to Britain, or whether all trade was conducted by way of middlemen on the Continent. On the face of it the latter seems most likely. The scatter of products of East Mediterranean origin indicates two major trade routes, one through eastern and central Europe to Germany (and perhaps to Britain), the other via Narbonne, Carcassonne and the Loire.

The travels of amber are but one of the clues for this Mediterranean connection. Mycenaean bronze double axes and copies of them have been found in Ireland and in England, datable to the period *c.* 1450–1220 BC, and a piece of an Aegean sword of the same date turned up at Pelynt in Cornwall. The stone battle axes that turn up in early Bronze

169

Age graves may owe some debt to Mediterranean double axes, while three gold earrings from Normanton, Folkestone and Dover are best matched in Minoan Crete. Other examples of early Bronze Age gold-work may owe something to Mediterranean inspiration. More intriguing still are the faience beads that have been found in many British Bronze Age barrows. Faience is a blue glass frit, distinctive of ancient Egypt, and battles have raged in academic circles over the question of whether the British

90 This superb necklace of jet was found at Poltalloch, Argyll. The spacer plates have designs pecked on them that reproduce the pattern of the threads stringing them. Similar necklaces of amber beads were traded from Britain to the Bronze Age east Mediterranean world. It recalls the lunulae of earlier times

finds are imports from the eastern Mediterranean or are native British products. If they are the latter, how did it come about that natives in the backwoods of Britain should devise on their own the sophisticated technology necessary to make faience and then fashion it into beads identical in shape and size to those from the sunny Mediterranean? A recent spectrographic study has attempted to show once and for all that the beads are of eastern origin, and compare with those found in the period 1500–1400 BC or somewhat later at sites such as Abydos in Egypt and Lachish in Syria but its conclusions have not been accepted and the latest suggestion is that they are Central European. A faience bead from a Wessex-style barrow at Earl's Barton, Northampton-shire, was dated on radio-carbon evidence to c. 1410 BC. This would tie in well with the Mediterranean evidence, which associates them with the XVIII Dynasty in Egypt. That they came direct from Egypt is unlikely – in view of the occurrence of amber in Egyptian graves at this time perhaps they were traded for northern amber through Mycenaean middlemen. From Wessex they may have been traded to

Scotland, where they have been found in graves of around the same period.

Most puzzling of all are the carvings of 'Mycenaean' daggers on one of the stones of the Stonehenge circle of trilithons. They have led theorists to suppose Stonehenge was master-minded by a Mycenaean architect. This is most unlikely, since Stonehenge was being erected, and the early Wessex culture was flourishing, before Mycenae existed. The great Lion Gate has been seen as the model for the Stone-

91 Carvings on sarsen stone 53, Stonehenge. Discovered in 1953, they have been inter-preted as representing a Mycenaean-type dagger (*left*) and a flat bronze axe (*right*). More recent opinion, how-ever, favours the view that the dagger is in fact a local Wessex type

henge trilithons but it was not built until the Wessex culture was at least a century and a half old. This does not mean the carvings were not of Mycenaean daggers, added to the stones when they were already standing, but recent studies of dagger pommels in Britain has indicated that the Stonehenge carvings may be of native weapons after all. They are weathered and probably never were very precise, so the truth about them may never be learned.

Behind the Wessex trade-links with the Mediterranean lies something more complex. This is not the kind of trade that nowadays brings Japanese transistor radios to Britain, but part of a more complicated network of relations. Objects such as the double axes may well have been ritual pieces, diplomatic objects whose value in the world of the Wessex chiefs was one of prestige and ritual. Theirs was a world in

171

which only a few centuries before stone axes had played some mysterious role in the cult of the sun. There is no doubt that Wessex chiefs saw some symbolic significance in axes – this would account for the other axe carvings at Stonehenge and on a slab from Badbury Barrow, Dorset.

Such carvings can be seen further afield in early Bronze Age Britain. In Argyll they adorn the slabs of a cist burial at Nether Largie and another nearby at Ri Cruin. In the early Bronze Age monuments of the Kilmartin area of Argyll other

92 Gold-bound amber disc and gold mount with criss-cross decoration from a Wessex chieftain's burial at Normanton, not far from Stonehenge, Wilts. Similar gold-bound amber discs have been found in Bronze Age Greece, where they arrived in trade

clues attest links with Wessex. From Badden has come a grooved and rebated slab of a cist, decorated with lozenge patterns like those of the Bush Barrow gold plates. The grooved and rebated technique is copied from wood-working, and recalls the tongue-and-groove and tenon-and-mortice jointing of the stones of Stonehenge. Although the amber necklaces are absent, jet takes their place, and one

93 Cup fashioned from a single lump of amber, found in a Wessex-style burial at Hove, Sussex. It is 8.9 cm in diameter, and was associated with a bronze dagger and stone battle axe in a tree-trunk coffin. Diameter 64.13 cm

of the Argyll cist burials has yielded a jet necklace of a mastery that would have been the envy of any Victorian craftsman from Whitby. Kilmartin has its standing stones, and another Wessex-style feature of the area is its linear cemetery, burials being laid in a line of barrows traversing the landscape.

Argyll, Brittany, Egypt, Mycenae – how much further afield did Wessex connections reach? Although the amber may have come from East Anglia, it is more likely to have

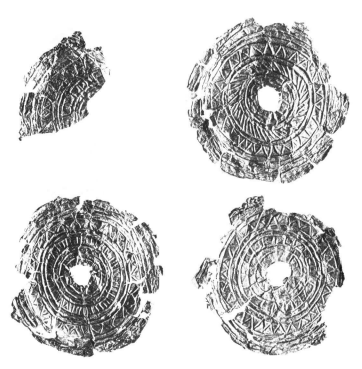

94 Gold 'sun-discs', perhaps attached to clothing, from one of the barrows known as the Knowes of Trotty, Mainland, Orkney

originated on Scandinavian shores, traded by central European middlemen. From the brilliant precocious metal-working culture known as the Únětice in Czechoslovakia came copper objects – exotic pins and the occasional axe. From Ireland came raw materials, gold and copper, and perhaps some axes and halberds – daggers which were mounted at right-angles to their hafts. Dorset shale was fashioned not only into beads but into drinking cups, from which no doubt the Wessex chiefs drank beer and mead, and (if one dare surmise), wine from Mediterranean shores.

In the lands of the midnight sun, another sun – of Wessex – sparkled on the waters of Lochs Harray and

Stenness. The gold sun-discs from the Orcadian Knowes of Trotty have a Wessex air about them, while amber spacer plates from the same barrow cemetery point more clearly to a Wessex link. All around Stenness and Brodgar and their linking processional way, so reminiscent of Avebury or Stonehenge, can be seen a rash of barrows. Many are bell barrows, occupying the centre of a ring defined by an encircling ditch and berm. These are a Wessex type of grave, and they are further evidence for a 'Wessex' phase in Orkney. This could have been a parallel flourishing, or one connected with the aristocracy of the south.

Deverel-Rimbury ranchers

Around 1400 BC or slightly earlier another settlement pattern was being established in southern Britain. This marks the beginning of a lifestyle that lasted until the coming of Caesar. It is known as the Deverel-Rimbury culture, and spans the period down to around 1100 BC, or perhaps slightly later. In the Deverel-Rimbury settlements agriculture seems to have been more important than stock-raising. Barley predominated in the later Bronze Age grain harvest (amounting to about 80 per cent of it), emmer wheat making up the rest. A major breakthrough in the period was the discovery of winter sowing – 70 per cent of the barley was of the hulled variety, which can be winter-sown and which thus ensured a steady food supply all the year round. The increase in crops and food generally probably led to a population boom.

Fields were cultivated by cross-ploughing. Constant ploughing on a slope led to the formation of banks (lynchets), which were sometimes heightened to form field boundaries by dumping stones cleared off the land.

The Deverel-Rimbury people have been given their name from two classic sites in Dorset, where burials were found in the nineteenth century. A novel feature of their lifestyle was the custom of burying their dead in characteristic urns in unmarked cremation cemeteries. They also disposed of the deceased in specially constructed barrows, or in the sides of pre-existing mounds.

For a long time the Deverel-Rimbury culture was regarded as the result of a colonization of southern Britain by Continental Urnfielders. It is now clear, however, that it is not a uniform culture but a long tradition with native origins in the earlier Bronze Age. It may have been influenced at some stage by Continental contact.

95 Bucket urn of Deverel-Rimbury type, found in a barrow at Milborne St Andrews, Dorset. Such pots were fashionable in the middle Bronze Age in southern Britain, and replaced the various types of cinerary urn and food vessel that went out of fashion around 1000 BC. Height: 33.02 cm

The later Bronze Age

Soon after 1400 BC the light was going out for early Bronze Age Britain. If old men complained that it seemed wetter now than in their youth, they would probably have been right. The long summer was giving way to a rainy autumn, and with the changing climate everything that is distinctive of the earlier Bronze Age in Britain passed away. All the familiar pottery – cinerary urns and food vessels, beakers and pygmy cups disappear. Henges and stone circles were abandoned, barrows were seldom heaped up. Why should these changes have taken place? There is probably no one simple answer. A decline in the population would seem a sensible suggestion to account for the new way of life, though there is very little evidence for this, and there are more hints that the available farm land was decreasing.

It is clear that from 1200 BC onwards and certainly after 1000 BC the climate was deteriorating rapidly. Old areas of settlement were being flooded out and perhaps in addition to these troubles some of the old haunts were exhausted from over-cultivation and were being taken over by blanket bog. This in itself might explain a decline in population but it cannot explain the radical social changes that are implied by the evidence. No invasions can be produced to explain widespread slaughter, though it is not impossible that plague played an important part in reducing the population. A comparable situation in historic times might be that of medieval England, where radical changes were brought about through first wetter conditions in the thirteenth century and then the Black Death in the fourteenth.

We cannot therefore assume that the social changes represented by the abandonment of so many features of Bronze Age life were due entirely to a decline in population. Instead it seems more likely that the dwindling amount of farm land put pressure on the people, leading inevitably to

96 Basal looped spearhead of the middle Bronze Age from near Doune, Perthshire. Compare this with the early Bronze Age spearhead from Snowshill (plate 87) and the late Bronze Age spearhead in the Heathery Burn hoard (plate 105) which show how these weapons developed during the Bronze Age

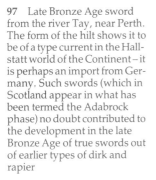

aggression. What evidence there is for late Bronze Age people suggests that they were notably warlike.

For the first time, in the late Bronze Age it is possible to kit out a fearsome warrior. Partly as a result of contact with the Continent, swords evolved out of rapiers during the period. Any late Bronze Age hero would have carried a leaf-shaped bronze sword cast in one piece, its hilt formed of plates of bone or wood kept in place by flanges. Spearheads too looked as spearheads should, with cast sockets through which a pin could be driven to fasten them to their shafts. Rugged Bronze Age faces were shaved with bronze bifid razors. Shields of wood, leather and even bronze were in use, though most of the surviving metal examples were ritual objects made for offering to the gods. It has been demonstrated that they are considerably less effective as protection than those of leather. The Bronze Age warrior seems to have needed armour but rarely. A series of helmets, now lost, were reputedly found in a barrow at Ogmore Down in Glamorgan; these had their counterparts from Beitzsch in Germany, where the discovery was dated to the fifteenth century BC on account of its similarity to a Minoan find from a tomb near Knossos. Whatever their date, they are oddities, and can hardly have been regular wear in Bronze Age skirmishing parties. The warrior is but one of the features of the late Bronze Age which look at first sight more at home in the Celtic Iron Age. After about 1400 BC a new settlement pattern was emerging – a landscape of hill-forts and scattered farmsteads.

Hill-forts and Farmsteads

The beginnings of hilltop defence were traceable in Neolithic Britain (p. 98). In the early Bronze Age the first tentative steps were taken towards the creation of hill-forts of the type that were eventually a striking feature of Iron Age Britain. The earliest are hill-top palisaded enclosures such as that excavated at Mount Pleasant, Dorset. However, relatively early in the period banks and ditches were being thrown up, for example at Rams Hill (where they underlie the later Iron Age hill-fort) or at Norton Fitzwarren in Somerset. The idea of putting up banks and ditches may have come from early Bronze Age ranching: such earthworks, usually too slight to have been much use as defence, have been found even on fairly indefensible sites, for example at Shearplace Hill, Dorset. What seem to be ranches with complexes of slight banks for cattle droving have been found widespread in southern Britain and have been assigned to the middle part of the Bronze Age. Some 'ranch-like' earthworks underlie

97 Late Bronze Age sword from the river Tay, near Perth. The form of the hilt shows it to be of a type current in the Hallstatt world of the Continent – it is perhaps an import from Germany. Such swords (which in Scotland appear in what has been termed the Adabrock phase) no doubt contributed to the development in the late Bronze Age of true swords out of earlier types of dirk and rapier

massive Iron Age hill-forts such as that at Yarnbury in Wiltshire.

In the middle part of the Bronze Age the first true hill-forts were probably erected. Among the earliest for which there is evidence, is Dinorben in north Wales. Radio-carbon dates show that by the middle of the twelfth century BC this hilltop was girt by a sophisticated rampart composed of clay and rubble with timber rafts. Some kind of timber framing was also apparent at Grimthorpe in Yorkshire, where a

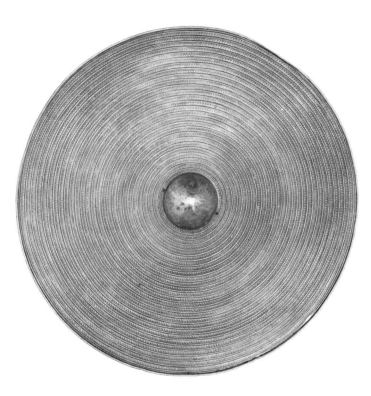

98 This superb bronze shield is one of a series from late Bronze Age Britain which were intended for ritual rather than practical use – they would not have stood up to combat, and the majority of real shields were probably of wood or leather. This example pro-claims the development of beaten metal-work in late Bronze Age Britain, and was found in a bog at Moel Siabod, near Capel Curig, Gwynedd, where it may have been placed as an offering to a god. Diameter: 64.13 cm

radio-carbon date suggested occupation as early as the late thirteenth century BC. Such hill-forts with timber lacing in the ramparts were fashionable on the Continent among Urnfield people. Perhaps it is not too much to suppose that Continental Urnfield influence was instrumental in the appearance of the forts in Britain – imported Urnfield bronze pins have been found on other similar sites (namely the Breiddin, Montgomery and Totternhoe in Bedfordshire).

In the later period of the Bronze Age hill-forts prolifer-ated, and several have produced hoards of stray metal-work of the time. They merge with the hill-forts built in the early Iron Age.

Settlements of the later Bronze Age

Until recently few settlements and very little pottery were assigned by archaeologists to the later Bronze Age, which was mainly studied through its metal-work. Now it is known that pottery once assigned to the very end of the Bronze Age and the beginning of the Iron Age belongs to the whole period of the later Bronze Age, from around the eleventh to the fifth centuries BC. In the first half of this period (from around the eleventh to the ninth century BC), prehistoric farmers were using thin-walled slab-built jars and bowls, some with vertical rippling on the exterior. In the latter part of the period, from the eighth century BC onwards, the pottery was much more richly decorated. It included some bowls coated with haematite to resemble metal, and other vessels with incised patterns originally filled with white 'inlay'.

Contemporaneous with the appearance of new types of pottery there were major social changes. Territorial divisions seem to have altered, and across the landscape of patchwork fields linear boundary ditches were driven. The precise nature of these is not yet properly understood, but they seem to be connected with territorial division. There is also evidence for an emerging system of markets and trade. Weapons were produced by professional smiths in the

99 Late Bronze Age stone hut circle, Grimspound, Dartmoor. In most parts of Britain houses were constructed of timber, but in the extreme south perhaps shortage of wood led to the building of such stone dwellings

Thames Valley and traded all over the country; minor products such as tools were produced locally to meet regional needs. On a regional level the markets are perhaps recognizable in some large sites such as Rams Hill, Berkshire, where the variety of pottery styles from neighbouring regions suggests that it served as a centre, not unlike the earlier 'causewayed camps', for communal activity and perhaps trade. On a more lowly level, there was a variety of farmsteads which carried on the tradition of the Deverel-Rimbury settlements, such as South Lodge on Cranborne Chase or Billingborough in Lincolnshire. Recent re-excavation of Down Farm (originally dug by Pitt-Rivers) has brought to light a rectangular building, 4m wide and at least 13m long. This is without parallel in Britain, but indicates that a rectangular building tradition as well as a tradition of round houses persisted throughout later prehistoric Britain.

In the northern highland areas of Britain a similar pattern became established in the late Bronze Age which also persisted through the Iron Age. The circular farmsteads that were scattered across the landscape were enclosed in palisades rather than ditches. None of these can be dated much before the eighth century BC and most are notably later. The time-lag may be explained by the fact that climatic deterioration had a more marked effect on the Highland Zone where depopulation in the late Bronze Age may have been quite extensive.

It is to the Northern Isles that scholars must turn for well attested evidence of settlement in the last few centuries of the Bronze Age. Here at sites such as Jarlshof and Clickhimin in Shetland, stone-built courtyard houses were the norm, furnished in some measure with stone fittings in the absence of wood. At Jarlshof cattle were stalled inside the dwelling. In one house a whalebone ring for tethering was set in the wall. A hollow in the floor of one dwelling was probably for the collection of manure – the earliest instance of the gathering of fertilizer in Britain. The need to stall animals indoors was probably the outcome of the colder, wetter conditions. Pastoralism was more important in the Northern Isles than agriculture.

Around the seventh century BC a smith moved in to one of the Jarlshof houses and began casting somewhat old-fashioned bronzes. About 200 fragments of clay moulds for making axes, swords, a gouge, and a pin were found with a casting pit filled with clean sand.

There is one other phenomenon of the later Bronze Age that is worthy of comment. Large numbers of finds of bronze-work have come from rivers, notably the Thames. While a few may have been the result of losses from ships and quaysides (one of which has recently been excavated at Runnymede Bridge, Surrey, with substantial timber-work), most are more readily explicable in terms of votive offerings. Such offerings may indicate that a cult was growing up connected with water, perhaps precipitated by the increased flooding of many sites.

Indeed, the overall picture of later Bronze Age Britain is increasingly like that of the succeeding Iron Age, into which it merges.

Gold

It is certainly a strange circumstance that an elderly woman who had been to Mold to lead her husband home late at night from a public-house, should have seen or fancied, a spectre to have crossed the road before her to the identical mound of gravel, 'of unusual size, and clothed in a coat of gold, which shone like the sun', and that she should tell the story the next morning, many years ago, amongst others to the very person, Mr John Langford, whose workmen drew the treasure out of the prison-house.

In these words the serious pages of *Archaeologia* for 1836 record the discovery of the Mold Pectoral, one of the finest treasures of Bronze Age Britain.

If the later half of the Bronze Age is lacking in those important evidential standbys of prehistorians, graves and ritual monuments, it does not have a dearth of gold-work. Few pieces of gold are finer than this object (Plate 100) found with some amber beads in a north Wales barrow in 1833. The Mold Pectoral is a shoulder cape made from a single sheet of relatively thick gold. Its surface is covered with a rich repoussé pattern of ribs and bosses, perhaps intended to look like beads, which are so arranged that when worn they would have swept down in the front and up at the

100 The Mold Pectoral, a sheet-gold cape found in a barrow in 1833 near Mold, Clwyd. Datable to around 1000 BC or slightly earlier, it is one of the earliest pieces of beaten gold-work from northern Europe, and is richly decorated with repoussé ornament to imitate the folds of cloth. Strangely, the best parallels for such shoulder capes come from ancient Egypt

shoulders, like the fall of cloth. At the back it was strength-ened with bronze strips, and it was probably sewn on to cloth or leather. Datable to around 1000 BC or slightly earlier, it is the first of a series of such pieces of beaten gold-work from prehistoric Europe. Intriguingly, the best paral-lels for similar shoulder capes come from ancient Egypt.

Most of the gold on which the Bronze Age craftsmen depended probably came from Ireland, where some of the finest examples of the goldsmith's art can be found. In

101 Twisted gold armlet from Stanton, Staffordshire. On such armlets folded bars were soldered apex to apex and then twisted to produce a scintil-lating effect – a device perhaps originating in Mediterranean lands. This was probably made in Ireland

Britain, the most superb examples are twisted necklets or torcs, of which the best is arguably that found at Moulsford near the Thames in Berkshire. Four bars of square section have each been twisted separately then put together, their ends contained in caps made from single sheets the sides and ends of which have been engraved to produce a varied linear effect. The torc weighs over a pound, and was made probably around 1400 BC. The twisted bar effect was an introduction around this time from east of the Rhine, where it was being used to great effect in central Europe. Of the same period and slightly later are a series of armlets the maker of which also used the twisted bar device to obtain a scintillating effect. On larger objects a round bar was grooved and then flanges hammered up from it, except for the ends, which were left plain. The effect thus produced on twisting was considerably more varied than was achieved with a plain twisted bar. For smaller, lighter gold objects two rectangular strips of sheet gold were folded down the centre then soldered back to back, so that four strips stood out

181

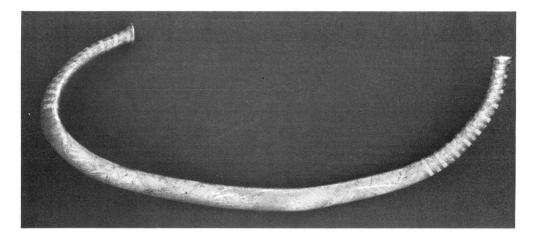

102 Gold torc or necklet found at Ickleton, Cambridge-shire in 1971. It is richly decorated with chevron orna-ment, and is of a type found in northern Europe, from where it was probably exported to Britain around the tenth century BC

at angles. They were then twisted. This device was of Mediterranean origin, and spread west via the Gulf of Lyons. Many of these gold objects must have adorned Bronze Age warriors, but others must surely have been made as offerings to the gods, such as the large torc from Ysgeifiog, Clwyd.

Among the smaller products of the goldsmith's art in the late Bronze Age were 'lock rings', penannular orna-ments perhaps for wearing in the hair. Some gold rings may have served as currency.

The end of the Bronze Age
The late Bronze Age was a time when trade and industry boomed and Britain was opened up after centuries of relative isolation to new influences from the Continent.

The major technological innovation of the time was the production of leaded bronze which facilitated finer castings. Numerous hoards of scrap metal can be assigned to the later part of the Bronze Age, and the various phases of the period have been named after important hoards. The picture that can be gained from the evidence is of smiths, with their bags of samples, collections of moulds and scrap metal, travelling tinker-like from farmstead to farmstead casting what was required at improvised forges. Just as stone axes had a symbolic value in Neolithic Britain, some bronze axes may have served a dual function in the centuries leading up to the Iron Age. Small axes are often found in hoards and may even have been a form of currency. In particular, certain types of square-socketed axes of Breton origin seem to have been too badly cast and made of too soft a metal to serve any practical purpose, and may have been the Bronze Age equivalent of coins.

103 Small socketed axes with loops, cast in bivalve moulds, are typical examples of the late Bronze Age smith's art. To see how far axes had developed since the beginning of the Bronze Age, compare plate 70

104 Stone axe moulds of the Bronze Age from Scotland. At the top is an open mould for casting axes of the type represented in plate 70; the mould in the centre with its 'cast' is a bivalve one of the late Bronze Age. That at the bottom is for a transitional type of axe

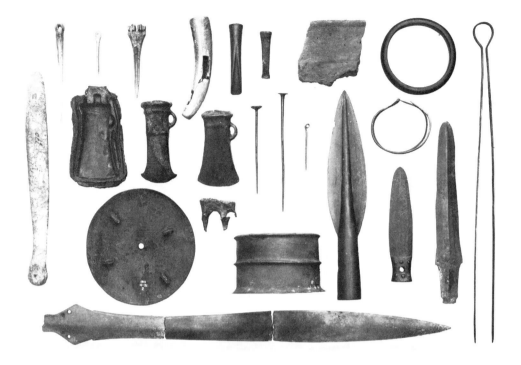

105 Part of a hoard from Heathery Burn Cave, Co. Durham, of the late Bronze Age. The objects are bone pins (*top row, 1–3*), antler cheek piece from horse harness, socketed gouge, socketed chisel, potsherd, lignite bracelet, bone spatula (*second row, far left*), axe mould and two axes, three bronze pins, spearhead (length: 25.14 cm), 'Sussex loop' (*above*) and socketed and tanged knives (*below*), tongs (*far right*). The three objects immediately above the sword at the bottom are a disc from a sword harness, a jet from a casting, and a bronze nave-band

Wessex and south Wales, which had been prominent in the early Bronze Age, were eclipsed by the Midlands and north Wales along with (possibly) the Fen country, after 1400 BC. The pioneers of leaded bronze were the Wilburton smiths (named after a hoard from Cambridgeshire) who modelled some of their products on foreign imports from the end of the tenth to the middle of the eighth century BC. Southern Britain at this time was trading with France, but few Wilburton products travelled into northern Britain and Wales, which remained conservative.

In the middle of the eighth century BC vigorous trade with France opened up southern Britain to new influences. Bronze swords with narrowed points (Canon Greenwell's carp's tongue swords) were imported, and gave rise to British versions. Breton axes of the type already mentioned were among the imports, and these prompted many British types. It seems almost as though there was a 'Common Market' in bronze-work (and probably other commodities as well) among the peoples that bordered on the Atlantic.

A technological innovation which had been pioneered among the Urnfield people of the Continent also made its mark on Britain at this time. This was the production of beaten bronze-work. Such metal was used for buckets, cauldrons and ornamental shields in the mid-eighth century and later. These objects hint at far-flung links with the eastern Mediterranean. High-shouldered buckets known as the Kurd type were imported to Wales and Ireland from Urnfield Europe and here they were imitated. Cauldrons which had been developed in the Mediterranean out of even more exotic oriental vessels appeared on British shores between 750 and 700 BC. These too were eagerly imitated for the market.

It is possible that the buckets were traded by Greeks who were in the habit of making a gift of such objects as a mark of high esteem. They could easily have been given to the inhabitants of southern France to build up good-will in their trading relations. Mediterranean cauldrons could then have travelled up an early version of the 'tin route' that operated in later Iron Age times. This would have followed the Rhône or perhaps the Atlantic Coast, from the Gulf of Lyons past Brittany. The trade was at any rate vigorous and may have been accompanied by the spread of a 'bull cult'. It is arguable that such a belief was attested in Ireland by the discovery of

106 Bronze armlets, necklet (*top centre*) and bifid bronze razor (*inside necklet*; length 8.89 cm) from a hoard found at Braes of Gight, Aberdeen-shire, with two further necklets (*bottom extreme left and right*). The hoard dates from *c.* 700 BC, and the armlets and necklets are probably imported from northern Europe.

107 Swan's-necked sun-flower pin used for fastening clothing in late Bronze Age Scotland. From Loch Broom, Ross

108 Beaten bronze-work of the late Bronze Age. The cauldron on the left (diameter 51.51 cm) was found in the Thames near Battersea, the bucket (height 44.7 cm) came from Heathery Burn Cave, Co. Durham, along with the other objects illustrated in plate 105. Beaten metal-work was a speciality of late Bronze Age smiths, and the inspiration behind such vessels was probably Mediterranean

a 'crotal' (a bell-like percussion instrument whose shape is supposed by some to be modelled on that of a bull's scrotum) in a late Bronze Age hoard from Dowris, Co. Offaly. Cauldrons apparently retained some of their Mediterranean mystique well into the Iron Age. They have sometimes been found as part of late Bronze Age offerings at lakesides, suggesting that the Iron Age custom of making offerings to water gods may be traced back into this period.

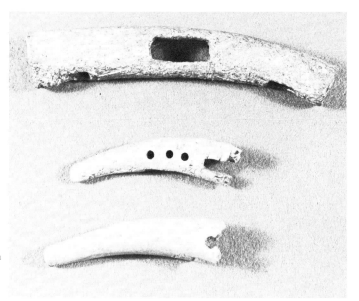

109 Antler cheek pieces from a late Bronze Age find at Runnymede Bridge, Surrey, 1976. Dating from around the seventh century BC, they came to light along with late Bronze Age metal-work and pottery on a settlement site. They attest the arrival of horse riding in late Bronze Age Britain

Epilogue

In 1910–11 work was in progress on the draining of Llyn Fawr, a lake in a peaty mountain tarn some 365.8m above Ordnance datum, in Glamorganshire. It was a bleak spot, overshadowed by a steep precipice and surrounded by a circle of rocky slopes. To reach the Glamorgan plain would have required an arduous journey across the high, wind-swept plateau and its deep trough valleys, and, should any coastal arrival have been seeking such an inhospitable place, he would have needed to travel some 21km on foot. Yet this journey was made by some person, or in all likelihood some family, in the middle of the seventh century BC, for they left behind a hoard of twenty-three (perhaps originally more) bronze and iron objects.

The Llyn Fawr hoard, as it is known, casts a shaft of light on the shadowy divide between the Bronze and Iron Ages. Many of the objects might seem typical of the late Bronze Age. There are two fine beaten bronze cauldrons, a series of six socketed bronze axes, three bronze chisels or gouges, an assortment of bronze sickles, and a bronze razor. But the razor is no ordinary Bronze Age bifid type. Instead it is a single-edged example of the kind found on the Continent among the Hallstatt Celts of Burgundy. The other objects are more unusual still. The most interesting are a series of iron items – a spearhead, a ferrous copy of one of the native bronze sickles, and part of a sword of Hallstatt Continental type, its hilt composed of bone plates rivetted to the tang. It perhaps came from Burgundy. The spearhead could be local but might equally well be a Continental import. The other bronze objects are undoubtedly exotic – two bronze pony cheek pieces, three bronze discs or 'phalerae' from harness decorations, an open-work harness mount and a belt hook. These pieces of horse gear are very similar to items found at Court St Etienne in Belgium in a Celtic Hallstatt cemetery.

The conclusions to be drawn are unmistakable. Taken as a group all the exotic objects were types current among the Celts in Belgium and southern Germany in the late seventh century BC. Almost certainly, they were brought to late Bronze Age Wales by an immigrant or immigrants of this date. It is plain that they brought with them the first ironwork to be seen in Britain. That they also taught the natives how to work iron is apparent from the fact that the sickle was of a type not found on the Continent. It was a purely local tool that had been made in the 'new' metal.

The items of horse harness attest something else that was fairly new in prehistoric Britain – horse riding. From late Bronze Age contexts have come a series of bits and other items of riding gear which show that now the mounted warrior was an enemy to be reckoned with. The Llyn Fawr horse gear was particularly interesting, for it was clearly imported and belonged to a class which is often termed 'Thraco-Cimmerian'. The Cimmerians were a horde of wild horsemen from the steppe-lands of Asia, who swept down through Europe and who seem to have been responsible for the spread both of horse riding and of iron technology. Here, in this quiet corner of Wales, the early Iron Age can be seen taking place.

The immigrants whose belongings were found at Llyn Fawr were undoubtedly Celts. Were they the first Celts in Britain? The question is unanswerable, since the term 'Celt' denotes a speaker of the Celtic language, and is not indicative of race or culture. The Hallstatt people of Continental Europe undoubtedly spoke a form of Celtic which was not far removed from that spoken in Britain in historic times; that is clear from the evidence of placenames. Since they were the direct descendants of the Urnfield people, it is inherently likely that some primitive form of

110 The Llyn Fawr hoard, Glamorgan. This hoard chronicles the divide between the Bronze and Iron Ages in Britain. The cauldron (*far left*) can be compared with that in plate 108. At the top (*centre*) is part of a Hallstatt Iron Age sword (length 26.5 cm), with an iron Hallstatt spearhead beneath. At the far right (*top*) are bronze phalerae from horse harness, similar to horse gear found in Hallstatt cemeteries on the Continent. In the centre, just above the bronze socketed gouge in the bottom row, can be seen an imported Hallstatt razor. The winged objects next to the cauldron in the centre are sword chapes, and the objects in the bottom right of the picture are sickles

Celtic was spoken in Britain by a few immigrants at least from the middle Bronze Age onwards. Use of a primitive dialect is, however, hardly sufficient for us to speak of 'Bronze Age Celts' in Britain, as some have done. Celtic Iron Age Britain begins with Llyn Fawr.

Bronze Age Britain did not end thus. The appearance of scattered groups of Celtic Hallstatt incomers did little to alter the native way of life, which continued for centuries to blend with the new fashions that blew across the Channel like the winds. The winds of change kept blowing until the arrival of Caesar, who found a Celtic Britain markedly different from Celtic Gaul. Its difference lay in the differing lifestyles of Bronze Age Britain and France.

The growth of British culture can be likened to a river with many tributaries: new influences are all the time flowing in to add to the mainstream, which grows and cascades through the pages of prehistory and history. No wave of invaders, whether Celts, Romans, Saxons, Vikings, Normans or far-off Beaker people totally changed the underlying pattern of traditions and life. Some made major contributions to British culture, some minor, but in retrospect all can be seen as blending in to a much more basic pattern that changes but slowly and which pays little heed to political upheavals.

Britons often find it difficult to appreciate how insular and insignificant the story of their island is when viewed against the wider backdrop of world or even European history. It cannot be stressed too strongly that Britain was the edge of the inhabited world, an inhospitable land, much of it difficult to tame, all of it subject to inclement weather – except perhaps in the 'long hot summer' of the Neolithic and early Bronze Age; a land in which the rapid dissemination of new ideas was made difficult by such geographical obstacles as the great mountain spine separating east from west, and surrounded by dangerous and treacherous seas which made the dissemination of ideas from the Continent difficult in the extreme. The Thames may have served as a communications artery for the south, and indeed, the innovatory character of southern Britain in antiquity reflects this well, but Britain has no Rhine or Danube along which ideas and men can travel with ease. Its interest lies not in its cultural brilliance, but in the fact that it is a cultural backwater of Europe, where old traditions die hard and can be observed in the process of change. It is not a random chance that Celtic culture survived in Britain to come under the spotlight of documentary history centuries after it had been snuffed out under the boot of Rome in Continental Europe.

But now and again in the long saga one can pick out a glimmer of something special. The Bronze Age Wessex of Stonehenge was one period at which Britain contributed to European culture, and Wessex was to contribute again in late Saxon times. In these fleeting instants in time one can glimpse what might have been, before conservatism swept all before it.

It is possible that not only the seeds of the Iron Age settlement pattern and economy can be traced back to late Bronze Age Britain, but the elements of Iron Age religion and tribal organization also. One authority has pointed out that the distribution of certain types of Bronze Age object corresponds closely with that of Iron Age tribes – one type of socketed axe found in Yorkshire matches in its distribution the territory of the Brigantes, while in Wales the land of the Silures coincides with the area in which the south Welsh type of axe is found. What are known as 'late palstaves' are mainly confined to the territory of the Ordovices, while the north Marches lands of the Cornovii coincide with the Bronze Age Broadward tradition. In Cornwall, the Trevisker style of late Bronze Age pottery coincides with the lands of the Dumnonii.

If an example of persisting tradition is required, one need look no further than the examples of prehistoric religious sites which have been deliberately 'converted' to Christianity. At Yspytty Cynfyn in Cardiganshire a church stands within a circular yard, a common enough device in Celtic Britain, and one which betrays a Dark Age origin for the site. Yet no ordinary vallum encloses the churchyard: the stone wall follows the bank of a prehistoric circle, and incorporates into it three of the original megalithic standing stones. If this might seem a fortuitous example, there are other examples of 'Christianized' megaliths. Twenty miles from Yspytty Cynfyn at Llanfairpwllgwyngell a standing stone lay beneath the pulpit of the church, while in north Wales at Gwytherin a line of four prehistoric standing stones can still be seen in the churchyard, one of them converted to use as a tombstone in the fifth century. These sites have their English counterparts. At Knowlton in Dorset a church stands within a henge monument. The first church on the site seems to date from the twelfth century, and represents a medieval attempt to render the site harmless – a group of twenty-six barrows (destroyed in the nineteenth century) stood nearby. The old gods of Britain still lurk in the shadows cast by the products of twentieth-century technology.

Appendix: Dating

The societies described in this book are all prehistoric, and by very definition this means they existed before recorded dates. Much of the story of prehistoric archaeology is the story of the quest for more accurate dates, and the quest still goes on. The discovery of the rate of decay of the radioactive isotope of carbon and the development of 'radio-carbon dating' from 1950 onwards (see p. 31) represented a major step forward in the working out of a chronology for Europe's prehistoric past. But discoveries in the 1960s led prehistorians to believe that the radio-carbon dates they were using were too 'young' in calendrical terms, and this has led to a 'second radio-carbon revolution' in which the established dates have been pushed back. Unfortunately, prehistorians are not all in agreement about exactly how the existing radio-carbon dates should be 'recalibrated' to give calendrical dates, and different 'calibration tables' exist to this end. Nor are all prehistorians happy about all the recalibrated dates, and tend to adjust them to what seems to them a more reasonable figure. It is now customary in archaeological literature to express dates in their 'uncalibrated' form, followed by bc or ad to indicate that they are radio-carbon years, not calendrical years that are being given. This number is then followed by a figure indicating the date bracket into which the date should fall, a reference provided by the laboratory which furnished the date and, finally, a 'recalibrated' date in brackets. Thus a date for Ballynagilly, Co. Tyrone, the earliest Neolithic site so far excavated, would read 3795 ± 90 bc (UB 305) (4580 BC). Such a system seemed to us too cumbersome and confusing for what is intended as a general introduction to early British prehistory, and instead the dates we have given are recalibrated dates in calendrical years. Where official recalibrations are not available, we have recalibrated the dates ourselves. All dates have been expressed in a round figure, and readers should bear in mind that they have been included simply to provide a relative time scale against which the cultural developments must be viewed. Dates prior to the upper Palaeolithic (around 60,000 BC) are not based on radio-carbon, but on other dating methods. No attempt has been made to recalibrate dates prior to 5000 BC, as the problems are as yet too great.

The best of early prehistoric Britain

This gazetteer lists fifty of the very best visible remains of early prehistoric Britain, arranged geographically.

Site	County	OS Grid Ref.	Description
Carn Brea	Cornwall	SW 686407	Neolithic hilltop settlement
Chun Quoit	Cornwall	SW 402339	Megalithic tomb chamber
Grimspound	Devon	SX 701809	Bronze Age hut
Stanton Drew	Somerset	ST 601633	Stone circle
Avebury	Wilts.	SU 103700	Stone circle, avenue of stones
Windmill Hill	Wilts.	SU 087714	Neolithic 'causewayed camp'
West Kennet	Wilts.	SU 104677	Megalithic tomb
Silbury Hill	Wilts.	SU 100685	Ritual Neolithic mound
Stonehenge	Wilts.	SU 123422	Neolithic and Bronze Age ritual site
Woodhenge	Wilts.	SU 150434	Neolithic ritual site
Belas Knap	Glos.	SP 020253	Megalithic tomb
Wayland's Smithy	Berks.	SU 281854	Megalithic tomb
Rollright Stones	Oxford	SP 296309	Stone circle
Kit's Coty House	Kent	TQ 745608	Megalithic tomb
Grimes Graves	Norfolk	TL 817898	Neolithic flint mines
Arbor Low	Derbys.	SK 161636	Henge
Bridestones	Yorks.	NZ 850046	Stone circle
Castlerigg	Cumbria	NY 291236	Stone circle
Long Meg and her Daughters	Cumbria	NY 571373	Stone circle
Barclodiad y Gawres	Anglesey	SH 328708	Megalithic tomb
Bryn Celli Dhu	Anglesey	SH 507702	Megalithic tomb
Dyffryn Ardudwy	Gwynedd	SH 587233	Megalithic tomb
Tŷ Isaf	Brecknock	SO 182291	Megalithic tomb
Drumtroddan	Wigtown	NX 363447	Cup-marked stone
Cairn Holy	Kirkcudbright	NX 518541	Megalithic tomb
Cairnpapple	West Lothian	NS 987718	Henge, stone circle, Bronze Age cairn
Loanhead	Aberdeen	NJ 748288	Recumbent stone circle
Nether Largie	Argyll	NR 832985, NR 831984 and NR 829980	Bronze Age linear cemetery
Temple Wood	Argyll	NR 826979	Stone circle with Bronze Age burial
Ri Cruin	Argyll	NR 825972	Bronze Age cairn
Clava	Inverness	NH 756445	Megalithic cairn
Camster	Caithness	ND 260443	Megalithic cairns
Hill o' Many Stanes	Caithness	ND 295384	Rows of standing stones
Callanish	Lewis	NB 213331	Stone circle, cairn
Maes Howe	Orkney	HY 318128	Megalithic tomb
Unstan	Orkney	HY 283117	Megalithic tomb
Brodgar	Orkney	HY 294134	Stone circle, henge
Stenness	Orkney	HY 306126	Stone circle, henge
Skara Brae	Orkney	HY 231188	Neolithic village
Cuween	Orkney	HY 364128	Megalithic tomb
Wideford	Orkney	HY 409122	Megalithic tomb
Dwarfie Stane	Orkney	HY 244005	Rock-cut tomb
Midhowe	Orkney	HY 372306	Megalithic tomb
Knowe of Yarso	Orkney	HY 403281	Megalithic tomb
Taversöe Tuick	Orkney	HY 426276	Megalithic tomb
Quoyness	Orkney	HY 677378	Megalithic tomb
Knap O' Howar	Orkney	HY 483519	Neolithic houses
Holm of Papa Westray	Orkney	HY 509518	Megalithic tomb
Stanydale	Shetland	HU 285503	'Temple'

Further reading

General books on British prehistory are mostly out of date – the classics were all published in the 1940s. The current standard introduction is C. Renfrew (ed.), *British Prehistory* (London, 1974), but it is poorly illustrated and very difficult to read for the non-specialist, as it is obsessed with the new radio-carbon dates and their implications. As an antidote S. Thomas, *Pre-Roman Britain* (London, 1965) is ideal, as it is a collection of 320 superb photographs with explanatory captions and a very short introduction. Of the older works, V. G. Childe, *Prehistoric Communities of the British Isles* (London, 1940) may be singled out. Two collections of essays cover Scotland and Wales respectively, and are both useful if somewhat specialist. They are S. Piggott (ed.), *Prehistoric Peoples of Scotland* (London, 1962) and I. Foster and G. Daniel, *Prehistoric and Early Wales* (London, 1965). The British Museum publication *Later Prehistoric Antiquities of the British Isles* (London, 1953) has useful illustrations. For environment, the best study is J. G. Evans, *The Environment of Early Man in the British Isles* (London, 1975). For the Continental background, S. Piggott, *Ancient Europe* (Edinburgh, 1965) and S. Piggott and J. G. D. Clark, *Prehistoric Societies* (London, 1965) are both first-rate, though now slightly out of date. The new edition of an earlier classic, J. G. D. Clark, *World Prehistory: a New Outline* (London, 1977) is valuable.

Antiquaries
The most informative books are all by Glyn Daniel. They are *The Origins and Growth of Archaeology* (Harmondsworth, 1967), *The Idea of Prehistory* (London and Harmondsworth, 1962), and *150 Years of Archaeology* (London, 1975). A fascinating collection of extracts can be found in R. Jessup, *Curiosities of British Archaeology* (Chichester 1974). S. Piggott, *Ruins in a Landscape* (Edinburgh, 1976) has interesting studies of particular themes. Key biographies of individual archaeologists and antiquaries are M. W. Thompson, *General Pitt-Rivers* (Bradford on Avon, 1978); S. Piggott, *William Stukeley* (Oxford, 1950); R. E. M. Wheeler, *Still Digging* (London, 1955); O. G. S. Crawford, *Said and Done* (London, 1955). Among earlier studies, T. Kendrick, *British Antiquity* (London, 1950), stands out.

Palaeolithic and Mesolithic
Unfortunately there is no recent survey of Palaeolithic and Mesolithic Britain. For human origins, a recent, if partisan, account is to be found in R. Leakey and R. Lewin, *Origins* (London, 1977). J. M. Coles and E. S. Higgs, *The Archaeology of Early Man* (London, 1969; paperback edn Harmondsworth, 1975), is a first-rate introduction to the stone industries of the Palaeolithic. The classic study of upper Palaeolithic Britain, now very out of date, is D. Garrod, *The Upper Palaeolithic Age in Britain* (London, 1926). This has been superseded

by J. B. Campbell, *The Upper Palaeolithic of Britain* (Oxford, 1977). For the lower Palaeolithic the standard work, strictly for specialists, is J. Wymer, *Lower Palaeolithic Archaeology in Britain* (London, 1968). The 'standard' for the Mesolithic in Britain, again largely super-seded by later research, is J. G. D. Clark, *The Mesolithic Age in Britain* (London, 1932). The same author's *Star Carr* (London, 1974) is a classic excavation.

Neolithic

The classic account, once again out of date, is S. Piggott, *Neolithic Cultures of the British Isles* (Cambridge, 1954). Long barrows are dealt with in P. Ashbee, *The Earthen Long Barrow in Britain* (London, 1970). Megalithic tombs have collected an enormous literature round them. One of the best studies, but rather technical, is T. G. E. Powell (ed.), *Megalithic Enquiries in the West of Britain* (Liverpool, 1969). A useful short introduction, once again rather out of date, is G. Daniel, *The Megalith Builders of Western Europe* (2nd edn, London, 1962). Two divergent modern interpretations are put forward in C. Renfrew, *Before Civilization* (London, 1972; paperback edn Harmondsworth, 1976), and E. MacKie, *The Megalith Builders* (London, 1977). D. D. A. Simpson (ed.), *Economy and Settlement in Neolithic and Early Bronze Age Britain and Europe* (Leicester, 1971) is a good collection of studies on such topics as house types and causewayed camps.

Bronze Age

There are no all-embracing studies of Bronze Age Britain. Barrows and burials are dealt with in P. Ashbee, *The Bronze Age Round Barrow in Britain* (London, 1960). The classic study of stone circles is A. Burl, *The Stone Circles in the British Isles* (New Haven, 1976). A corpus of beakers along with one interpretation of them can be found in D. L. Clarke, *Beaker Pottery of Great Britain and Ireland* (London, 1970) – this is very technical for the non-specialist.

Index

Skara Brae, Orkney, 99, 101–4; carved stone balls at, 106; possible writing at, 104
Smith, Worthington, 55
sociological archaeology, 37
South Cadbury, Somerset, 35, 110
South Street, Wilts, field, 84–5
Stanydale, Shetland, 106–7
Star Carr, Yorkshire, 68–9; dog from, 72
Stenness, Stones of, Orkney, 159, 174
Stoke Newington, London, 55; forgers at, 75
Stonehenge, 117–20, 158, 164–6, 172
Storrs Moss, Lancs, 86
Stukeley, W., 9, 10, 11
Sutton, Glamorgan, 154
Swanscombe, Kent, 51, 54

Swanwick, Hants, 112
Sweet Track, Somerset, 86, 94–5
swords, late Bronze Age, 184

T
television, 33–4
Thatcham, Berks, 4
thermoluminescence, 36
Thomsen, C., 19
Three Age System, 19
tool-making, 45–6
Torbryan, Devon, 57
trade, Neolithic, 86–95
Triorweth, Anglesey, 154
Twyne, J., 4
typology, 21–2

U
Upton Lovell, 168
Urnfields, 177, 184–5

W
Walbrook, London, 33
Walton Track, Somerset, 95
Wayland's Smithy, Berks, 126–8
Wessex culture, 166–74; amber in, 168; trade with Mycenae, 169
West Kennet, Wilts, 123
Wheeler, Sir R. E. M., 27–8, 31, 33–4
Wilburton, Cambs, 184
Wilsford Shaft, Wilts, 110–12
Windmill Hill, Wilts, 110, 112, 113; animal and plant ratios at, 82
Windmill Hill Cave, Brixham, 16
Woodhenge, Wilts, 117
Wookey Hole, Somerset, 44, 58
Worsaae, J. J. A., 19

Y
Yadin, Y., 35